# A-Z BEDF

C000257403

## CONTENT

## REFERENCE

| | | | |
|---|---|---|---|
| A Road | A6 | Car Park (Selected) | P |
| Under Construction | | Church or Chapel | † |
| Proposed | | Cycleway (Selected) | 🚴 |
| B Road | B531 | Fire Station | ■ |
| Dual Carriageway | | Hospital | H |
| One-way Street | | House Numbers A & B Roads only | 298 77 |
| Traffic flow on A Roads is also indicated by a heavy line on the driver's left. | | Information Centre | i |
| Restricted Access | | National Grid Reference | 504 |
| Pedestrianized Road | | Park & Ride | Dart P+ |
| Track & Footpath | | Police Station | ▲ |
| Residential Walkway | | Post Office | ★ |
| Railway | Tunnel Station Level Crossing | Toilet: without facilities for the Disabled with facilities for the Disabled | ▽ ▽ |
| Built-up Area | DART / P.O. | Educational Establishment | |
| Local Authority Boundary | | Hospital or Hospice | |
| Posttown Boundary | | Industrial Building | |
| Postcode Boundary (within posttown) | | Leisure or Recreational Facility | |
| | | Place of Interest | |
| Map Continuation | 12 Large Scale Town Centre 52 | Public Building | |
| | | Shopping Centre or Market | |
| | | Other Selected Buildings | |

## SCALE

| Map Pages 4-51 | | | | Map Page 52 | | | |
|---|---|---|---|---|---|---|---|
| 1:15,840 | 4 inches (10.16cm) to 1 mile | | 6.31 cm to 1km | 1:7,920 | 8 inches (20.32 cm) to 1 mile | | 12.63 cm to 1km |
| 0 | ¼ | | ½ Mile | 0 | ⅛ | | ¼ Mile |
| 0 | 250 | 500 | 750 Metres | 0 | 100 | 200 | 300 Metres |

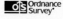

## Copyright of Geographers' A-Z Map Company Limited

Fairfield Road, Borough Green, Sevenoaks, Kent  TN15 8PP
Telephone:  01732 781000 (Enquiries & Trade Sales)
01732 783422 (Retail Sales)

www.a-zmaps.co.uk

Copyright © Geographers' A-Z Map Co. Ltd.

**Ordnance Survey** This product includes mapping data licensed from Ordnance Survey® with the permission of the Controller of Her Majesty's Stationery Office.

© Crown Copyright 2005. All rights reserved. Licence number 100017302

EDITION 1   2006

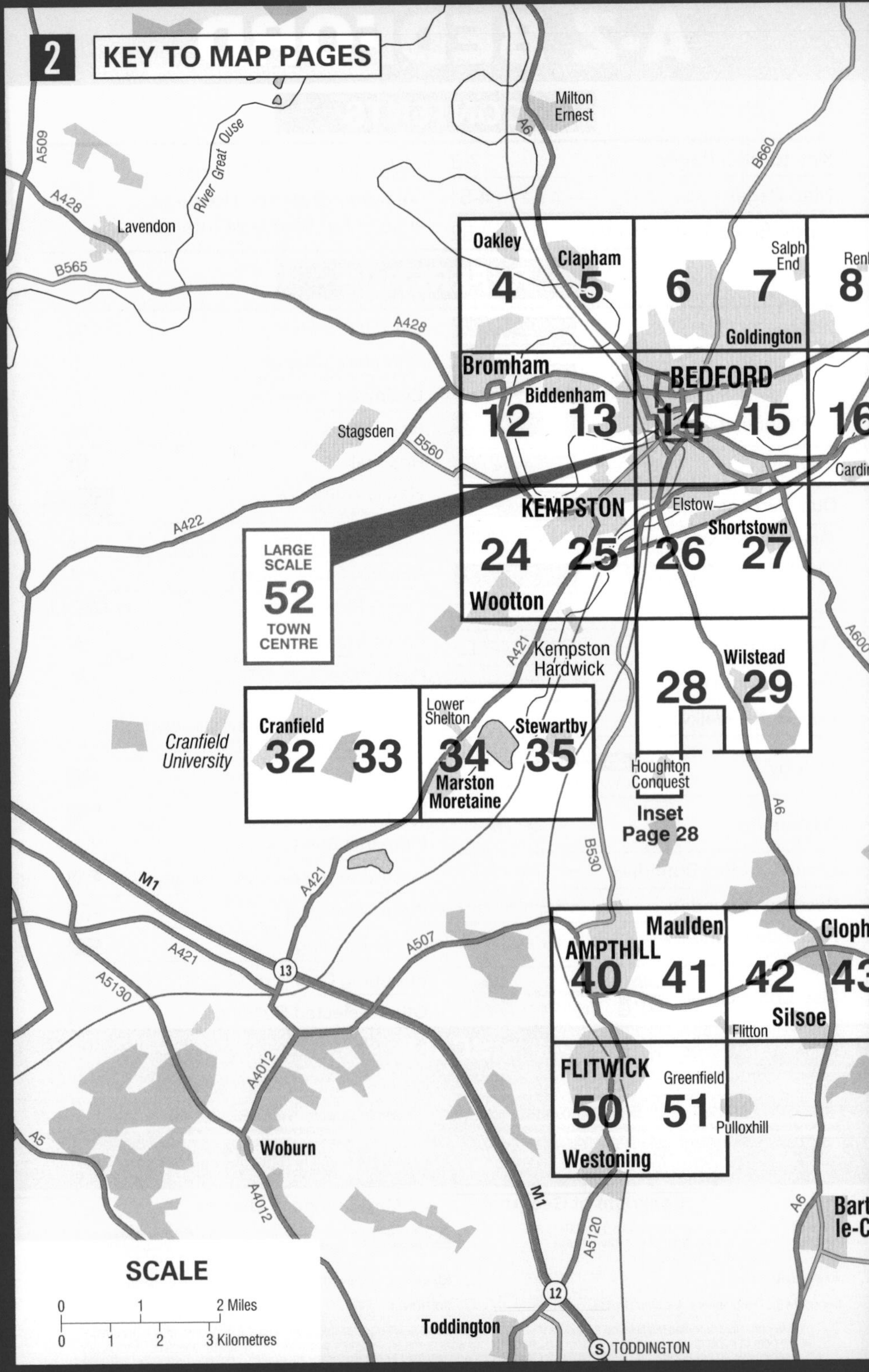

# 2 KEY TO MAP PAGES

Milton Ernest

Lavendon

River Great Ouse

A509
A428
B565
A428
A428
B660
A6
B560
A422
A421
A421
B530
B560
A507
A4012
A4012
A5130
A5
M1
A5120
A6
A600

Oakley **4** Clapham **5** **6** Salph End **7** Ren **8** Goldington

Bromham **12** Biddenham **13** **BEDFORD 14** **15** **16** Cardir

Stagsden

## LARGE SCALE **52** TOWN CENTRE

KEMPSTON **24** **25** **26** **27** Elstow Shortstown
Wootton

Kempston Hardwick **28** Wilstead **29**

Houghton Conquest

**Inset Page 28**

Cranfield University Cranfield **32** **33** Lower Shelton **34** **35** Stewartby
Marston Moretaine

Maulden
AMPTHILL **40** **41** **42** **43** Cloph
Silsoe
Flitton

FLITWICK **50** Greenfield **51** Pulloxhill
Westoning

Woburn

Bart le-C

## SCALE

0 — 1 — 2 Miles
0 — 1 — 2 — 3 Kilometres

**Toddington** (S) TODDINGTON

13

12

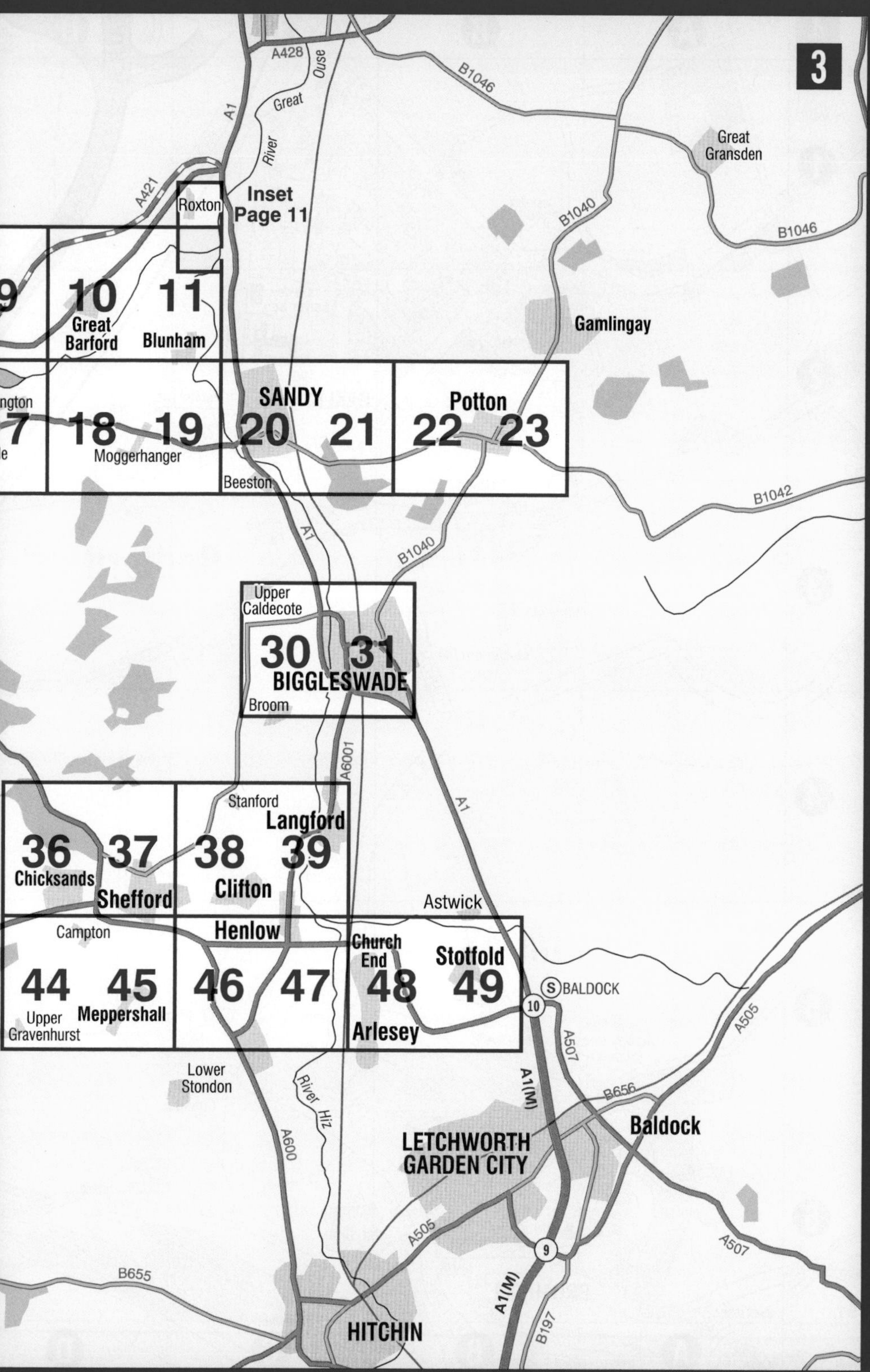

A428
Great Ouse River
A1
A421
B1046
Great Gransden
Roxton
Inset Page 11
B1040
B1046
9
10
Great Barford
11
Blunham
Gamlingay
ngton
SANDY
Potton
7
18
19
20
21
22
23
e
Moggerhanger
Beeston
B1042
A1
B1040
Upper Caldecote
30
31
BIGGLESWADE
Broom
A6001
A1
Stanford
Langford
36
37
38
39
Chicksands
Shefford
Clifton
Astwick
Campton
Henlow
Church End
Stotfold
44
45
46
47
48
49
S BALDOCK
10
Upper Gravenhurst
Meppershall
Arlesey
A507
A505
Lower Stondon
A1(M)
River Hiz
B656
Baldock
A600
LETCHWORTH GARDEN CITY
A505
9
A507
B655
A1(M)
B197
HITCHIN

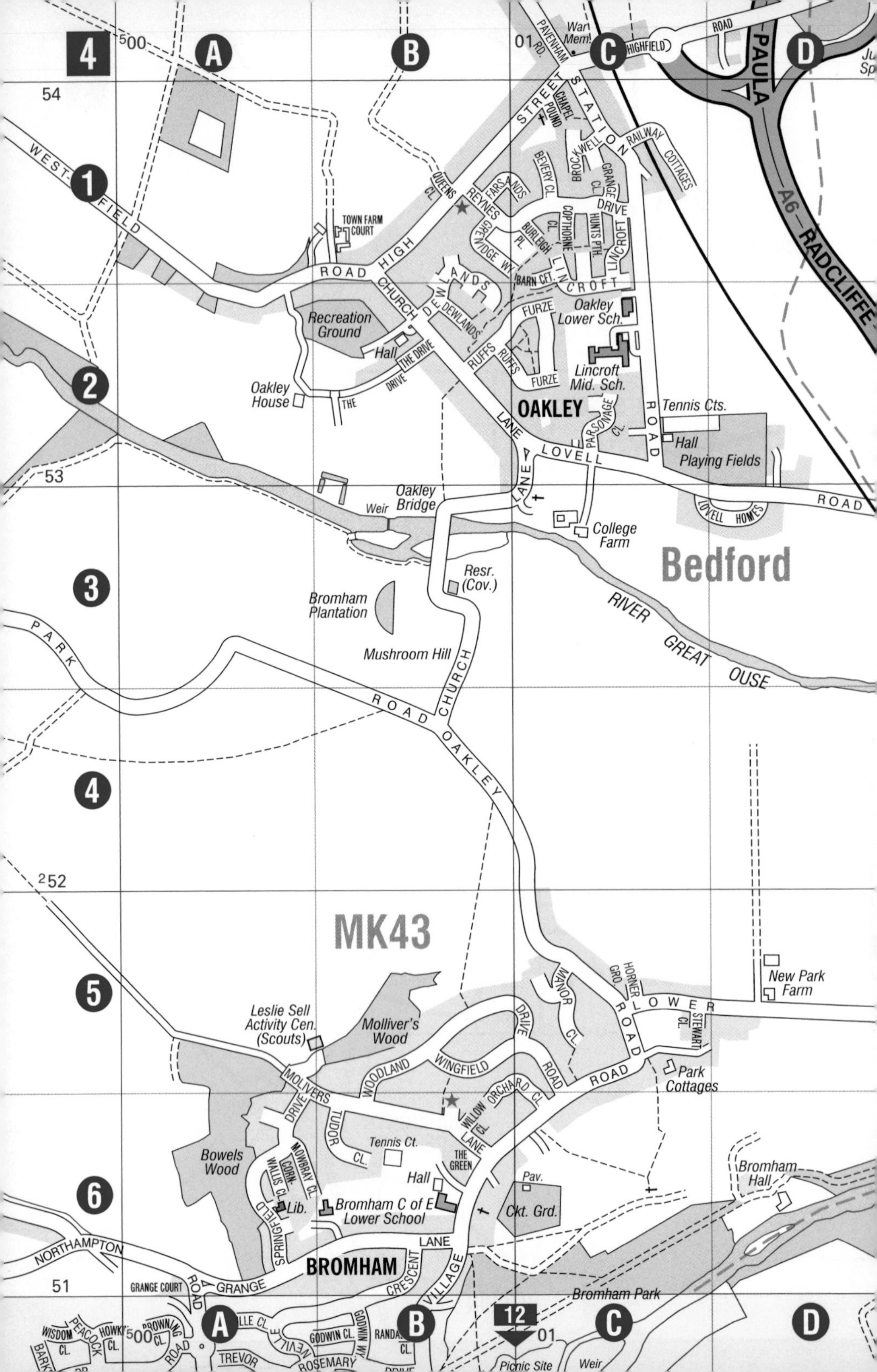

A
B
C
D
1
2
3
4
5
6
500
01
54
53
252
51
OAKLEY
Bedford
MK43
BROMHAM
WESTFIELD ROAD
HIGH STREET
STATION ROAD
HIGHFIELD ROAD
PAULA
A6 RADCLIFFE
PAVENHAM RD.
War Mem.
CHAPEL POUND
RAILWAY COTTAGES
BROCKWELL
BEVERY CL.
GRANGE CL.
DRIVE
QUEENS CL.
REYNES
FARSANDS
GRENIDGE WY.
PL.
BURLEIGH CL.
COPTHORNE
HUNTS PTH.
LINCROFT
BARN CFT.
TOWN FARM COURT
CHURCH
DEWLANDS
FURZE
RUFFS
Recreation Ground
Hall
THE DRIVE
Oakley House
Oakley Lower Sch.
Lincroft Mid. Sch.
PARSONAGE CL.
Tennis Cts.
Playing Fields
LANE
LOVELL ROAD
LOVELL HOMES
Oakley Bridge
Weir
College Farm
Resr. (Cov.)
Bromham Plantation
Mushroom Hill
RIVER GREAT OUSE
PARK ROAD
CHURCH
OAKLEY
MANOR CL.
HORNER GRO.
LOWER ROAD
STEWART CL.
New Park Farm
Park Cottages
Leslie Sell Activity Cen. (Scouts)
Molliver's Wood
MOLIVERS DRIVE
WOODLAND
WINGFIELD DRIVE
WILLOW LANE
ORCHARD CL.
TUDOR CL.
Tennis Ct.
THE GREEN
Bowels Wood
MOWBRAY CL.
CORN.
WALLIS CL.
SPRINGFIELD
Lib.
Bromham C of E Lower School
Pav.
Ckt. Grd.
Bromham Hall
NORTHAMPTON ROAD
GRANGE COURT
GRANGE
CRESCENT
VILLAGE
Bromham Park
12
WISDOM CL.
PEACOCK
HOWKIN CL.
BROWNING CL.
NEVILLE CL.
TREVOR
GODWIN CL.
GODWIN WAY
ROSEMARY DRIVE
RANDALL CL.
Picnic Site
Weir

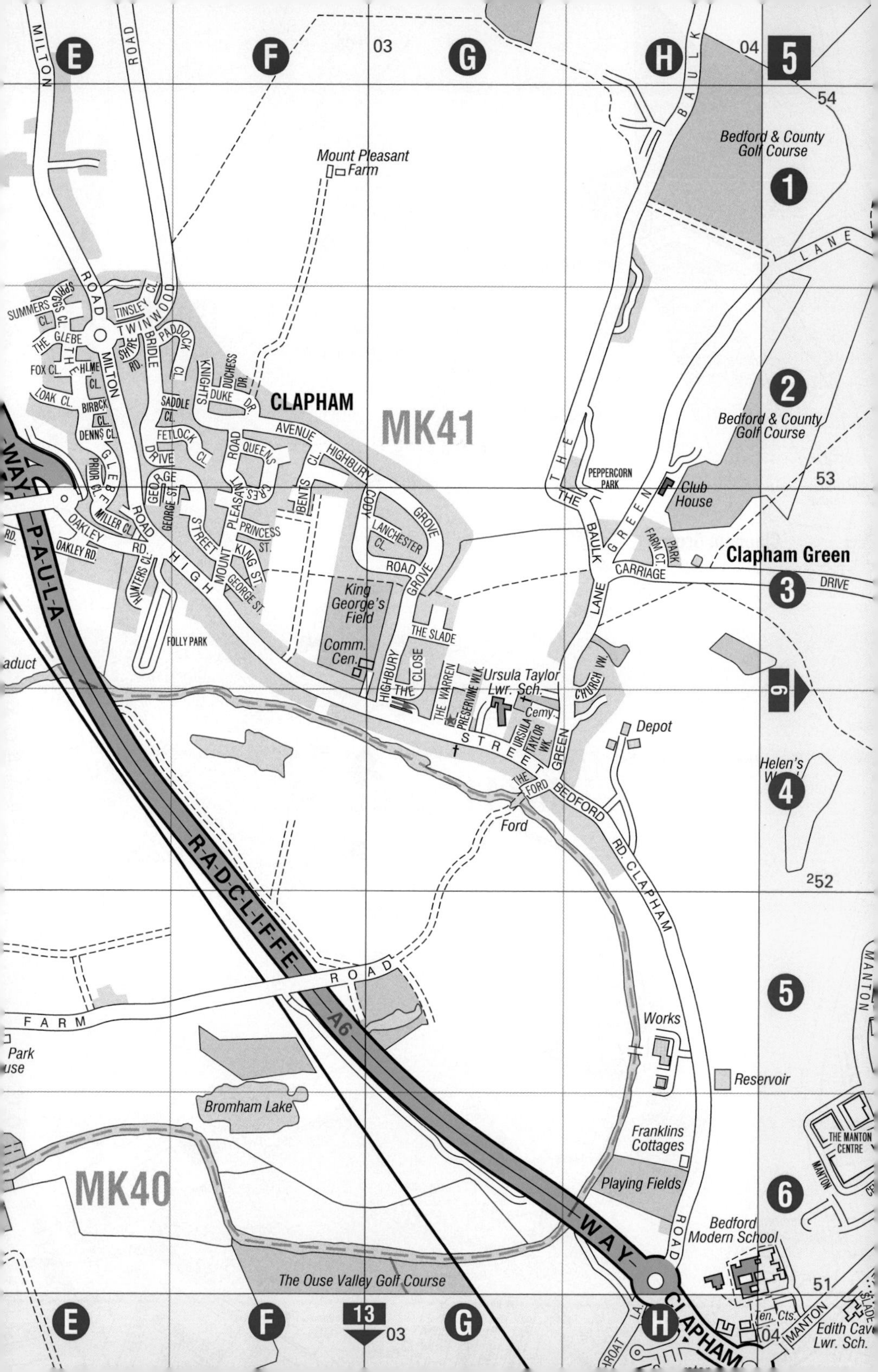

# Map: Clapham (MK41 / MK40)

E · F · 03 · G · H · 04 · **5** · 54

**1**

Bedford & County Golf Course

**2**

Bedford & County Golf Course · 53

Mount Pleasant Farm

SUMMERS CL · THE GLEBE · TINSLEY CL · TWINWOOD · PADDOCK CL · BRIDLE RD · SPRINGWOOD · MILTON ROAD · SHYRE CL · KNIGHTS CL · DUCHESS DR · DUKE DR

FOX CL · HLME CL · BIRBCK CL · SADDLE CL · FETLOCK CL · LOAK CL · DENNS CL · PRIOR RI · GLEBE RD

**CLAPHAM**

**MK41**

AVENUE · HIGHBURY GROVE · COBY RD · GROVE

GEORGE ST · QUEENS CRES · IBENTS CL · LANCHESTER CL

MILLER CL · OAKLEY RD · HUNTERS CL · HIGH STREET · MOUNT PLEASANT · KING ST · GEORGE ST · PRINCESS ST · KING GEORGE RD

THE BAULK · THE LANE · THE GREEN

PEPPERCORN PARK · Club House · PARK · FARM CT

**Clapham Green**

**3** · DRIVE · CARRIAGE

FOLLY PARK

King George's Field · Comm. Cen. · THE SLADE · THE CLOSE · THE WARREN · PRESERVINE WLK · HIGHBURY WK · URSULA TAYLOR WK

Ursula Taylor Lwr. Sch. · Cemy · CHURCH VW

**9**

Depot

Helen's Wood

**4** · 252

† · STREET · THE FORD · GREEN · BEDFORD RD CLAPHAM

Ford · Ford

P·A·U·L·A WAY · OAKLEY RD

R·A·D·C·L·I·F·F·E ROAD · A6

aduct

**5**

Works · □ Reservoir · MANTON

Park use · FARM

Bromham Lake

**MK40**

Franklins Cottages · THE MANTON CENTRE · MANTON

Playing Fields

**6** · 51

Bedford Modern School

WAY · CLAPHAM ROAD · THROAT LANE · Ten. Cts. · Edith Cave Lwr. Sch. · Edith Cave

The Ouse Valley Golf Course

E · F · **13** ▽ 03 · G · H · 04

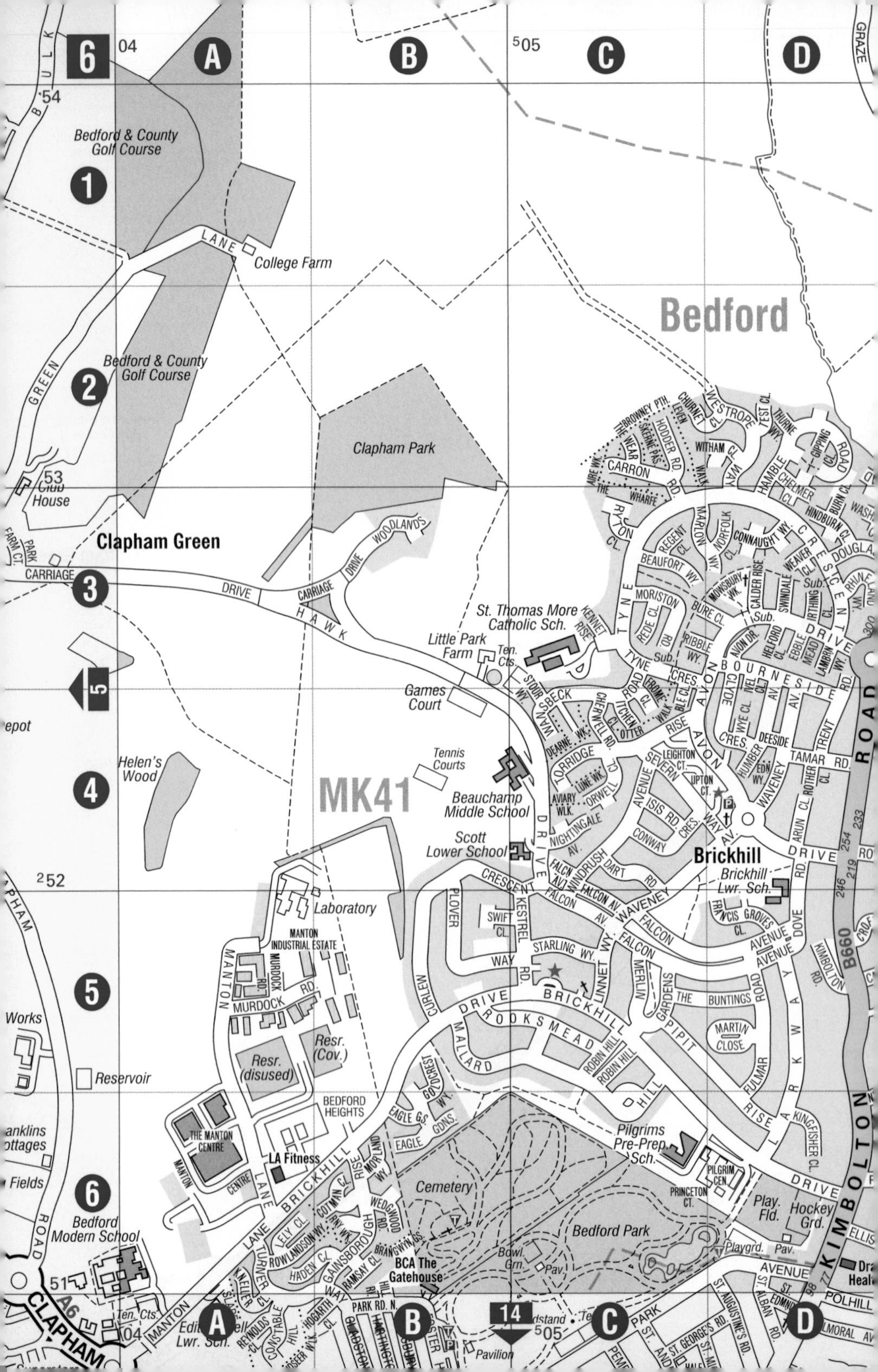

6
A
B
C
D
Bedford & County Golf Course
College Farm
Bedford
Clapham Park
Club House
Clapham Green
Carriage Drive
Hawk Drive
St. Thomas More Catholic Sch.
Little Park Farm
Games Court
Tennis Courts
Helen's Wood
MK41
Beauchamp Middle School
Scott Lower School
Brickhill
Brickhill Lwr. Sch.
Laboratory
Manton Industrial Estate
Resr. (disused)
Resr. (Cov.)
Reservoir
Works
Bedford Heights
The Manton Centre
LA Fitness
Cemetery
Bedford Park
Pilgrims Pre-Prep. Sch.
Play. Fld.
Hockey Grd.
Bedford Modern School
BCA The Gatehouse
Kimbolton Road
B660
Pavilion
14
5

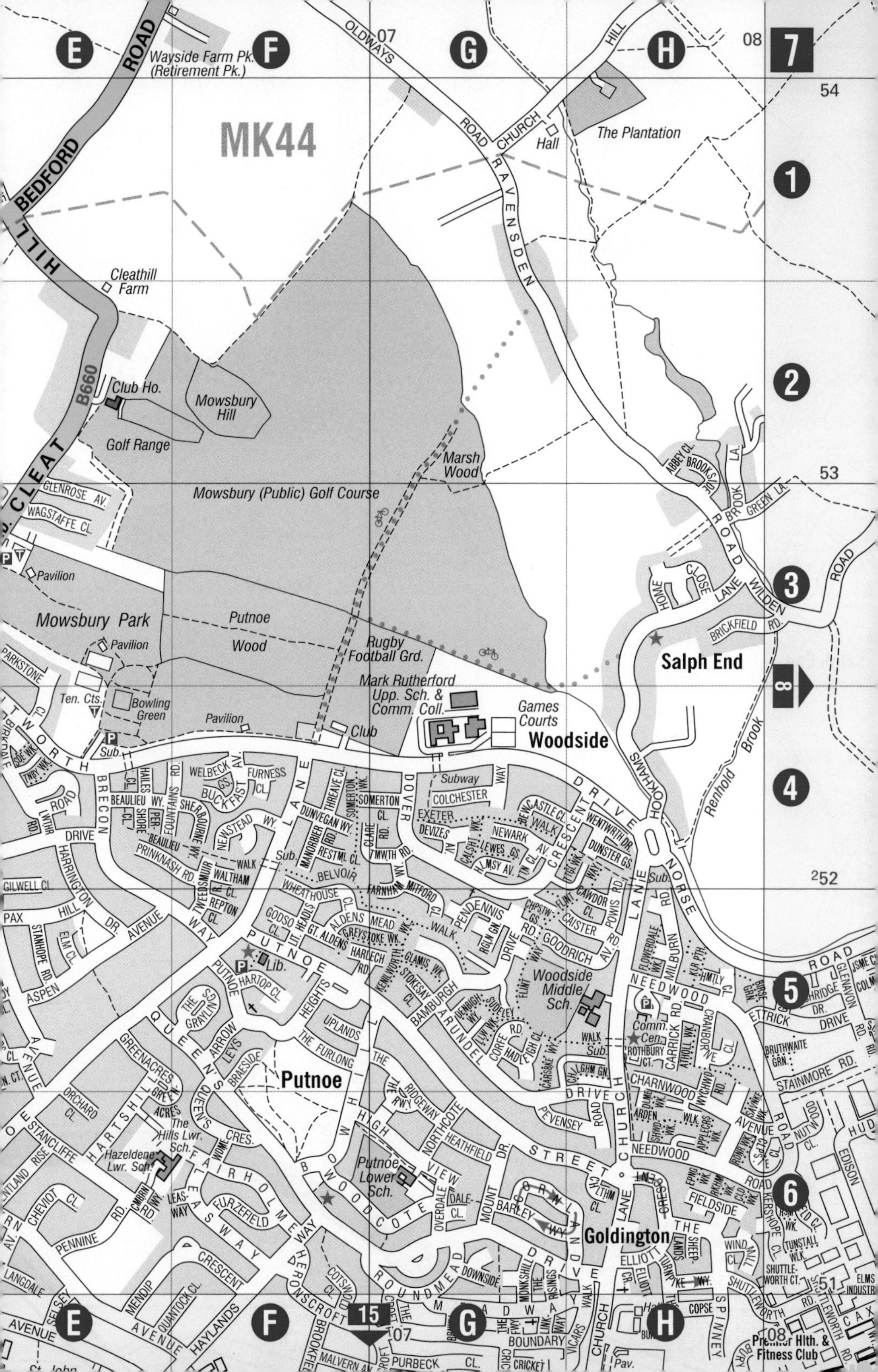

7
MK44
Wayside Farm Pk. (Retirement Pk.)
The Plantation
Hall
Cleathill Farm
Club Ho.
Mowsbury Hill
Golf Range
Marsh Wood
Mowsbury (Public) Golf Course
Pavilion
Mowsbury Park
Putnoe Wood
Rugby Football Grd.
Mark Rutherford Upp. Sch. & Comm. Coll.
Games Courts
Woodside
Salph End
Ten. Cts.
Bowling Green
Club
Subway
Woodside Middle Sch.
Comm. Cen.
Putnoe
Goldington
Putnoe Lower Sch.
The Hills Lwr. Sch.
Hazeldene Lwr. Sch.
Premier Hlth. & Fitness Club
Lib.
Renhold Brook
BEDFORD ROAD
CLEAT HILL
B660
OLDWAYS ROAD
CHURCH HILL
RAVENSDEN ROAD
WILDEN ROAD
BRICKFIELD RD.
HOOKHAMS LANE
NORSE ROAD
PUTNOE LANE
PUTNOE STREET
CHURCH LANE
GOLDINGTON ROAD
BOWHILL
WOODCOTE
ROUNDMEAD
MEADWAY
FAIRHOLME
LEASWAY
QUEENS DRIVE
HARTSHILL
ELMS INDUSTRIAL
15
8

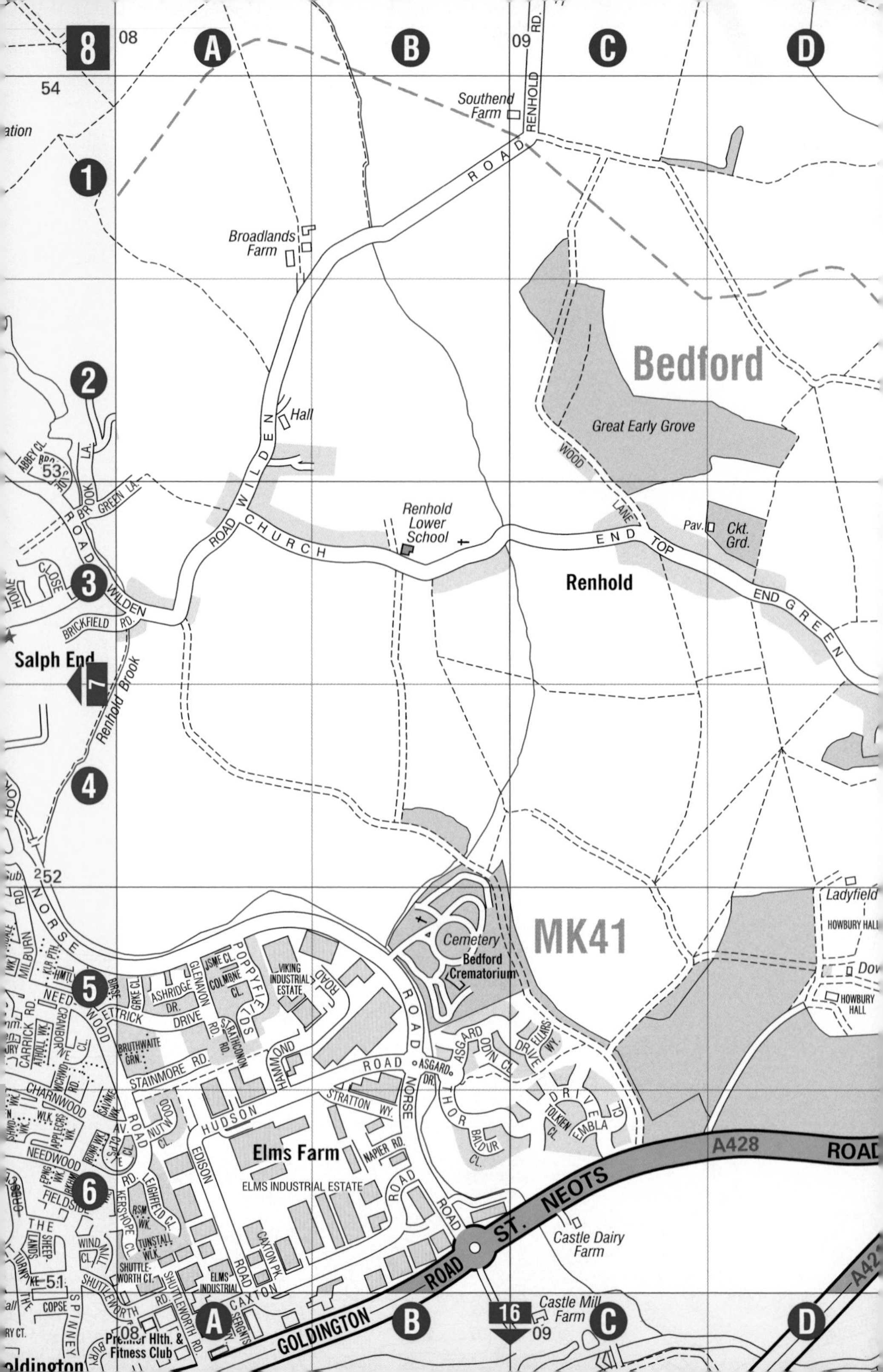

**8** 08

54

**A** **B** 09 **C** **D**

RENHOLD RD.

Southend Farm

ROAD

**1**

Broadlands Farm

**2**

53

WILDEN

Hall

BROOK GREEN LA.

LA.

ABBEY CL.

HOME CLOSE

WILDEN

ROAD

**Bedford**

Great Early Grove

WOOD

LANE

END

TOP

GREEN

END

Pav.

Ckt. Grd.

**Renhold**

ROAD

CHURCH

Renhold Lower School

**3**

BRICKFIELD RD.

**Salph End**

**7**

Renhold Brook

HOOK

**4**

252

NORSE

SUB

ROAD

MILBURN

WD. PTH.

NEEDHAM

CRANKEY

CARRICK RD.

BRET

FETTRICK

WOOD

**5**

ASHRIDGE DR.

ESME CL.

GLENAVON

POPPYFIELDS

COLMINE CL.

STAPLEFORD RD.

HAMMOND

Viking Industrial Estate

ROAD

Cemetery

Bedford Crematorium

**MK41**

ASGARD DRI.

ASGARD DR.

ODIN CL.

THOR

DRIVE

Ladyfield

HOWBURY HALL

Dov

HOWBURY HALL

BRUTHWAITE GRN.

STAINMORE RD.

CHARNWOOD

NEEDWOOD

**6**

CARRICK RD.

LEIGHFIELD CL.

ELM ELMS WY.

FOLKEN CL.

EMBLA CL.

BALDUR CL.

STRATTON WY.

NAPIER RD.

NORSE

ROAD

**Elms Farm**

ELMS INDUSTRIAL ESTATE

EDISON

HUDSON

CAXTON PL.

51

THE SHEPP

COPSE

SHUTTLEWORTH CT.

SPINNEY

ELMS INDUSTRIAL

SHUTTLEWORTH RD.

A428 ROAD

ST. NEOTS

Castle Dairy Farm

**A** 08 **B** **C** **D**

Premier Hlth. & Fitness Club

GOLDINGTON

ROAD

**16** 09

Castle Mill Farm

A42

oldington

9
E
F
G
H
11
12
54
53
52
51
1
2
3
4
5
6
10
17
BARFORD ROAD
BIRCHFIELD ROAD
BIRCHFIELD
Little Birchfield Farm
Northfield Farm
MK44
The Creakers
(Est. Comp. Late 2006)
Subway
Greenend Farm
GREEN END RD.
Playing Field
Pavilion
Woodfield Farm
WOODFIELD LA.
Workhouse End
GREAT BARFORD BY-PASS
Brewer's Hall Farm
WATER END
ST. NEOTS ROAD
BEDFORD ROAD
A421
WATER LANE
River Great Ouse
Gadsey Brook Cottage

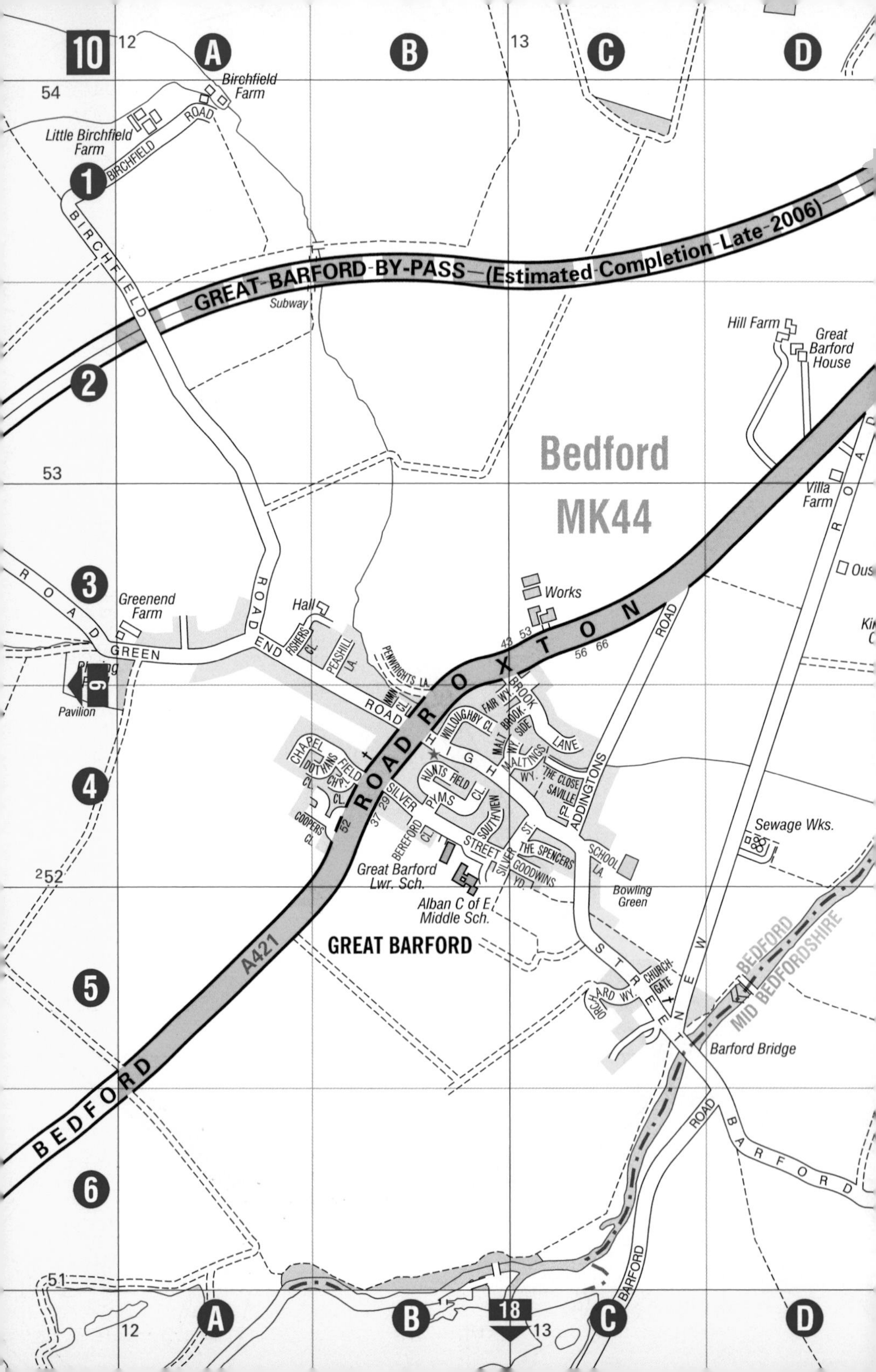

# 10

**Bedford**
**MK44**

**GREAT BARFORD BY-PASS** (Estimated Completion Late 2006)

Subway

Birchfield Farm

Little Birchfield Farm

BIRCHFIELD ROAD

Hill Farm

Great Barford House

Villa Farm

Ous

Ki

Greenend Farm

ROAD GREEN

Hall

ROAD END

Pewrights La.

Peashill La.

Works

ROXTON ROAD

Playing Field

Pavilion

ROAD

High

Willoughby Cl.

Fair Wy.

Mall Brook

Brook Side

Brook Lane

The Close

Saville Cl.

Addingtons

CHAPEL CL.

SILVER

Hants Field

Smith View

Maltings Wy.

School La.

Sewage Wks.

COOPERS CL.

BEDFORD ROAD

Great Barford Lwr. Sch.

Alban C of E Middle Sch.

Silver Street

Goodwins Yd.

The Spencers

Bowling Green

**GREAT BARFORD**

A421

BEDFORD

Church Gate

Street

New

Barford Bridge

BEDFORD / MID BEDFORDSHIRE

BARFORD ROAD

**18**

BARFORD

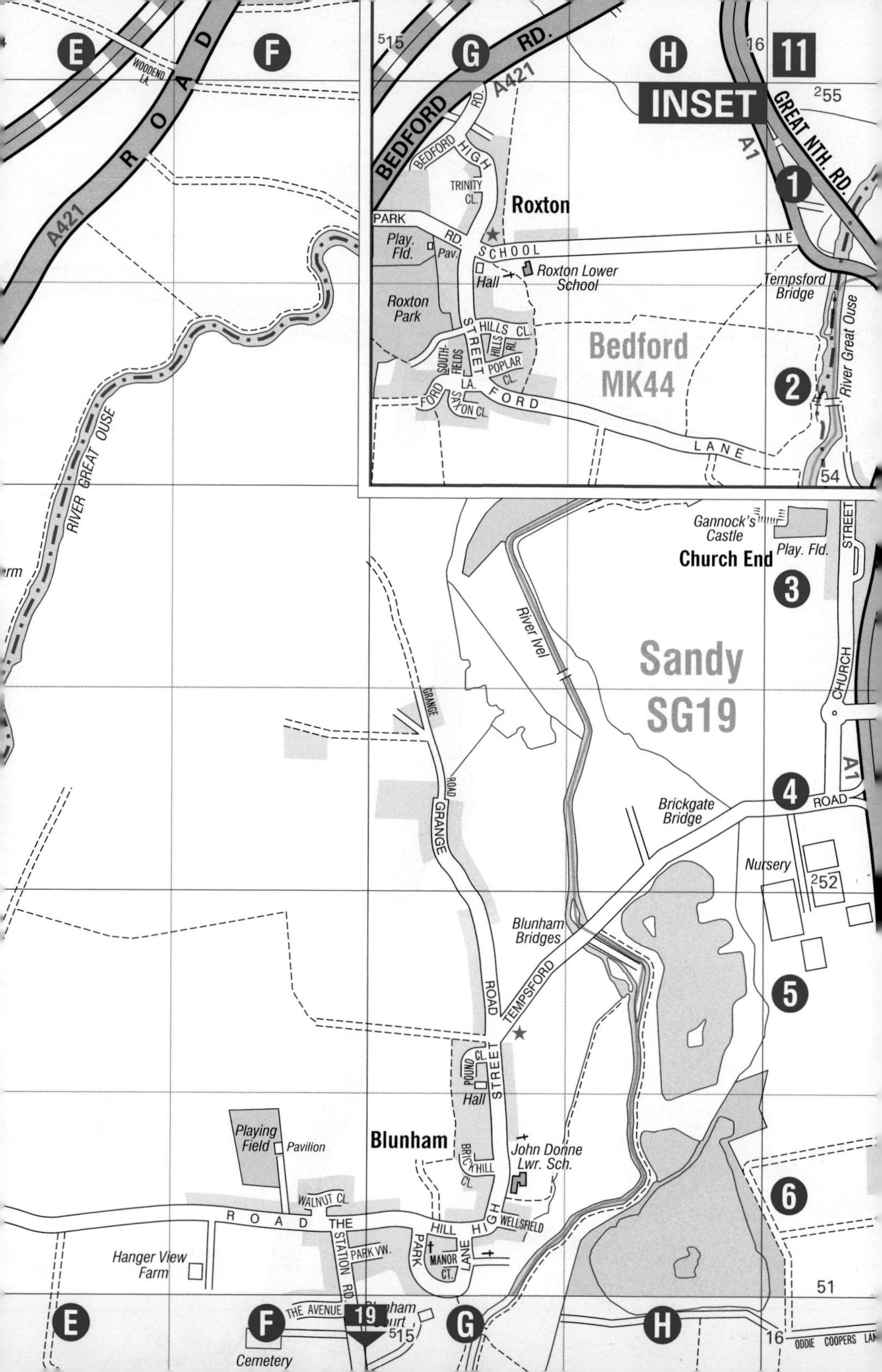

E · F · **G** · **H** · **11**

WOODEND CL.

R O A D

A421

BEDFORD RD.

A421

515

BEDFORD HIGH

A1

GREAT NTH. RD.

16

255

**INSET**

**1**

TRINITY CL.

BEDFORD

**Roxton**

LANE

PARK

Play. Fld.

SCHOOL RD.

Pav.

Hall

Roxton Lower School

Tempsford Bridge

**2**

Roxton Park

STREET

HILLS CL.

SOUTH-FIELDS

HILLS RI.

POPLAR CL.

FORD

River Great Ouse

Bedford MK44

FORD

LA.

SAXON CL.

F O R D

LANE

54

River Great Ouse

rm

River Great Ouse

Gannock's Castle

Play. Fld.

STREET

**Church End**

**3**

River Ivel

**Sandy SG19**

GRANGE

CHURCH

GRANGE ROAD

Brickgate Bridge

ROAD

**4**

252

Nursery

A1

Blunham Bridges

ROAD

TEMPSFORD

STREET

**5**

POUND CL.

Hall

John Donne Lwr. Sch.

**Blunham**

Playing Field

Pavilion

BRICK HILL CL.

HIGH

WALNUT CL.

R O A D

THE

STATION RD.

PARK

HILL

STREET

Wellsfield

**6**

51

PARK VW.

MANOR CT.

LANE

Hanger View Farm

THE AVENUE

**19**

515

Blunham Court

E · **F** · **G** · **H** · 16

Cemetery

ODDIE COOPERS LANE

Lower School
NORTHAMPTON
GRANGE
GRANGE COURT
LANE
ROAD
Bromham Park
4
NEVILLE CL.
CRESCENT
GODWIN CL.
GODWIN WY.
RANDALLS CL.
WISDOM
PEACOCK
HOWKIN CL.
BROWNING CL.
BARKER
DR.
TREVOR
ROSEMARY
DRIVE
Picnic Site
Weir
Bromham Mill & Gall.
Bromham Bridge
BROOK WAY
DRIVE
LEYS SIDE
WEBBS CL.
VILLAGE
BUCKS CL.
MILLFIELD
CEDAR CL.
HAWTHORN
WESTVIEW
DYNEVOR
PRINCES
BERRY
BROMHAM
STAGSDEN
ROAD
Bridge End
BROMHAM
RD.
BROOKSIDE PARK HOMES
PARTRIDGE
WALNUT
THE SPINNEY
LA.
STAGSDEN
ORCHID WY.
ROSE WK.
THISTLEY LA.
MAYHEW
BATCHELDOR
GDNS.
PINSENT AV.
QUENBY
LIME CL.
NEW
JACKMAN CL.
QUENBY WY.
BRETT
SYMONDS
CARTWT. CL.
DOVEHOUSE CL.
HERONS MEAD
THE PADDOCKS
DR.
Bedford
Ouse Valley Farm
BIDDENHAM
DUCK END LA.
LANE
GOLD
THE MANOR BMI HOSPITAL
A428
Swan Works
BOX
A5134
MK43
Moorland
CHURCH
CHURCH END
THE OLD BARNS
END
MANOR RD.
Hanger Wood
The Bedford Golf Course
DRIVE
PRESTWICK RD.
Club House
ST. MELLION
DRIVE
Crossland Farmhouse
Crossland Fosse
END
ROAD
RIVER GREAT OUSE
CARNOUSTIE
GREENKEEPERS RD.
KINGSWOOD
LYTHAM PL.
MUIRFIELD
STONE CL.
GREAT LIT. PORTWAY
PORTWAY
WAY
WHITINGS
WOODVILLE DR.
END
(Proposed)
Box End Farm
Rushey Ford Farm
WEST
West End Farm
WEST END R.
A5134
ROAD
B560
Vicarage Farm
Kempston Church End
Weir
24
Play. Fld.
Hall
CHURCH RD.
Kempston
A
B
C
D
1
2
3
4
5
6
500
01
51
50
49
48

MK41

MK40

MK42

The Ouse Valley Golf Course

BIDDENHAM GRANGE

BROMHAM

BIDDENHAM GRANGE

WINDMILL HILL

Club House

Playing Fields

The Alexander Sports Centre

Play Flds.

Tennis Courts

A428

BROMHAM ROAD

St. Gregory's RC Middle Sch.

Biddenham Upper School & Sports College

Tennis Courts

Westfield Mid. Sch.

St. Joseph's RC Lwr. School

Queen's Pk. Lwr. Sch.

Queen's Park

Barnfield Coll.

Hockey Pitch

Bedford Sports & Hockey Cen.

CHESTER

CARLISLE

Bowl. Grn.

The Bedford Golf Course

Allen Park Rec. Grd.

Pav.

OLD FORD

Sikh Tem.

Halls

Brewery

Gas Holders

Superstore

Bedford Modern School

HOSP.

Bedford

RIVER GREAT OUSE

Queen's Bridge

Football Grd.

Kempston Pool

Lawson Park Indoor Bowl. Club

St. John's Sch.

HILLGROUNDS

Canterbury Cl.

Westminster Gdns.

Comm. Cen.

Addison Howard Park

Grange School

Tennis Courts

Playground

THE GRANGE

Blenheim

Ind. Est.

Ind. Est.

KEMPSTON

Yth. Cen.

Robert Bruce Middle Sch.

14
6
52
13
26
BEDFORD
Bedford
Queen's Park
South End
River Great Ouse
Bedford Modern School
Edith Cavell Lwr. Sch.
Bedford Park
Robinson Pool
Bedford School
BEDFORD HOSP. (Nth. Wing)
BEDFORD HOSP. (Sth. Wing)
Bedford Blues RUFC
Bowling Club
Bedford College
County Hall
Shire Hall
Springs Sports Hall
Bedford St. Johns
Gas Holders
Brewery
Queen's Bridge
Cauldwell Lwr. Sch.
Shackleton Lwr. Sch.
Dame Alice Harpur Sch.
Castle Mound
Mus. Art Gall.
Bus Sta.
MIDLAND STRUCTURES INDUSTRIAL ESTATE
KINGFISHER BUS. PARK
FENLAKE ROAD IND. EST.
PIONEER PARK
Livingstone Lwr. Sch.
St. Bede's Sch.
Superstore
CLAPHAM ROAD
SHAKESPEARE RD.
BROMHAM ROAD
ASHBURNHAM RD.
TAVISTOCK ST.
GOLDINGTON
KIMBOLTON ROAD
HIGH STREET
PREBEND ST.
CAULDWELL ST.
KINGSWAY
ROPE WLK.
LONDON ROAD
KEMPSTON RD.
AMPTHILL RD.
ELSTOW ROAD
MILE ROAD
CASTLE ROAD
THE EMBANKMENT
A6
A428
A5141
A603
A600
A421
B531
B660
A5134
MK40
MK42

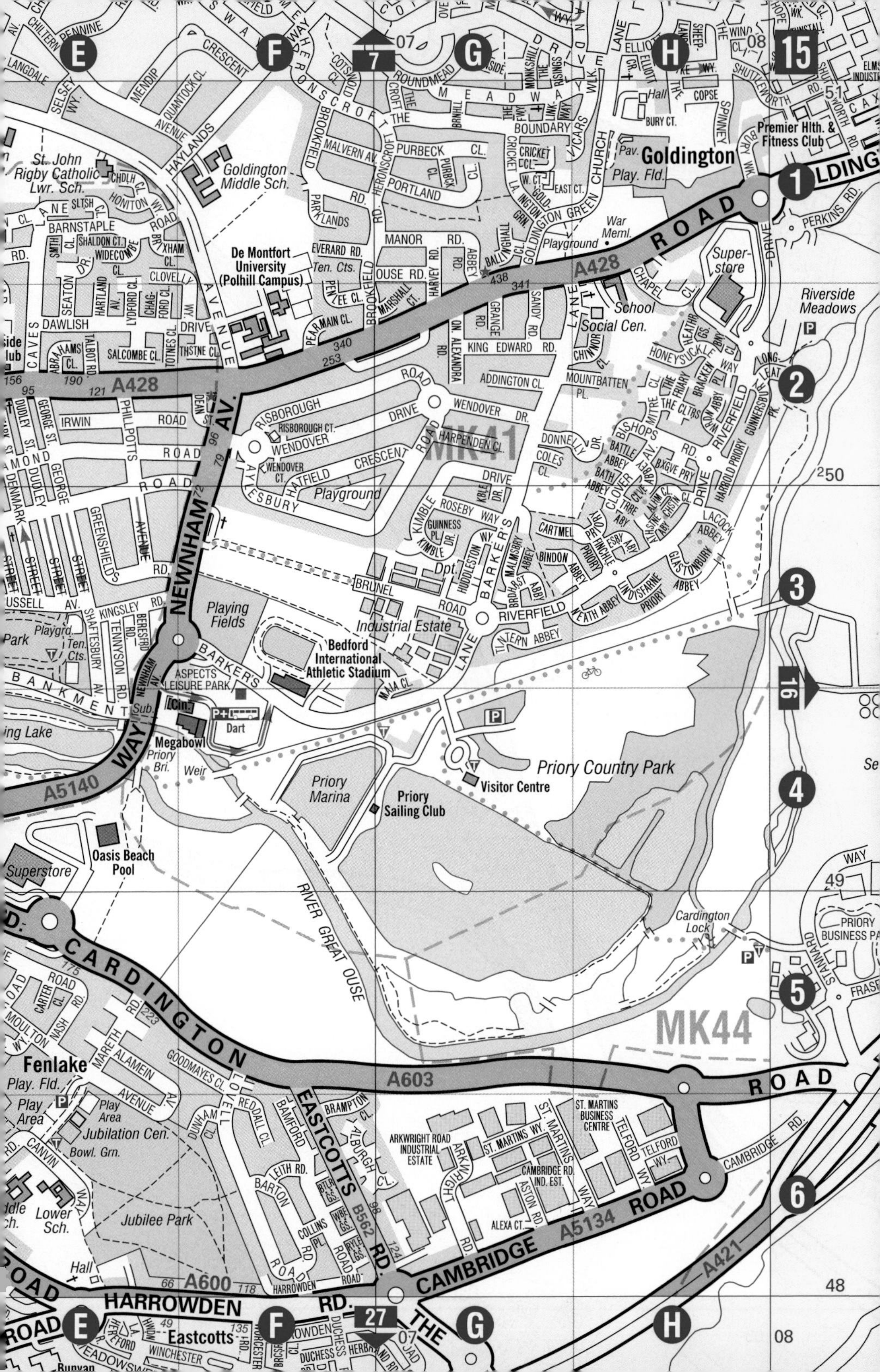

15
7
27
16
E
F
G
H
1
2
3
4
5
6
Goldington
Play. Fld.
Premier Hlth. & Fitness Club
St. John Rigby Catholic Lwr. Sch.
Goldington Middle Sch.
De Montfort University (Polhill Campus)
Superstore
Riverside Meadows
School
Social Cen.
War Meml.
Playground
MK41
MK44
Playing Fields
Industrial Estate
Bedford International Athletic Stadium
Aspects Leisure Park
Dart
Megabowl
Priory Bri.
Weir
Priory Marina
Priory Sailing Club
Visitor Centre
Priory Country Park
Oasis Beach Pool
River Great Ouse
Cardington Lock
Priory Business Park
Fenlake
Play. Fld.
Play Area
Jubilation Cen.
Bowl. Grn.
Jubilee Park
Lower Sch.
Hall
Eastcotts
Arkwright Road Industrial Estate
St. Martins Business Centre
Cambridge Rd. Ind. Est.
A428
Goldington Road
Newnham Av.
Newnham Way
A5140
Cardington Road
A603
Eastcotts Rd.
B562
Cambridge Road
A5134
A421
A600
Harrowden Rd.
Riverfield Drive
Barker's Lane
Brunel Road
Wendover Drive
Aylesbury Crescent
Hatfield Crescent
Risborough Road
Kimble Dr.
Roseby Way
Huddleston Wy.
Riverfield
Tintern Abbey
Lindisfarne Priory
Glastonbury Abbey
Lacock Abbey
Harrold Priory
Gunnersbury
Bishops Av.
Mitre Cl.
Mountbatten Pl.
Addington Cl.
King Edward Rd.
Sandy Rd.
Grange Rd.
Alexandra Rd.
Chapel Cl.
Goldington Green
Church Lane
Vicars Wlk.
Boundary
The Meadway
Purbeck Cl.
Portland Rd.
Manor Rd.
Heronscroft
Brookfield Rd.
Malvern Av.
Parklands
Everard Rd.
Ouse Rd.
Harvey Rd.
Marshall Ct.
Pearmain Cl.
Haylands
Quantock Cl.
Mendip
Crescent
Selsey Wy.
Chiltern
Pennine
Langdale
Barnstaple
Widecombe Cl.
Clovelly Wy.
Seaton Dr.
Hartland Av.
Lydford Cl.
Dawlish
Salcombe Cl.
Totnes Cl.
Caves Lane
Irwin Road
Philpotts Road
Dudley St.
George St.
Denmark Street
Greenshields
Kingsley Rd.
Tennyson Rd.
Shaftesbury Av.
Russell Av.
Embankment
Mareth Rd.
Alamein Avenue
Goodmayes Cl.
Lovell
Reddall Cl.
Dunham Cl.
Bamford
Brampton Cl.
Alburgh Cl.
Barton
Collins Pl.
Leith Rd.
Arkwright Rd.
St. Martins Wy.
Telford Wy.
Aston Rd.
Alexa Ct.
Carter Cl.
Nash Rd.
Moulton Wy.
Canvin Way
Winchester
Duchess
Stannard
Way
Frase
Perkins Rd.
Shuttleworth Rd.
Elliott Cr.
Copse
Spinney
Bury Ct.
Bury Wk.

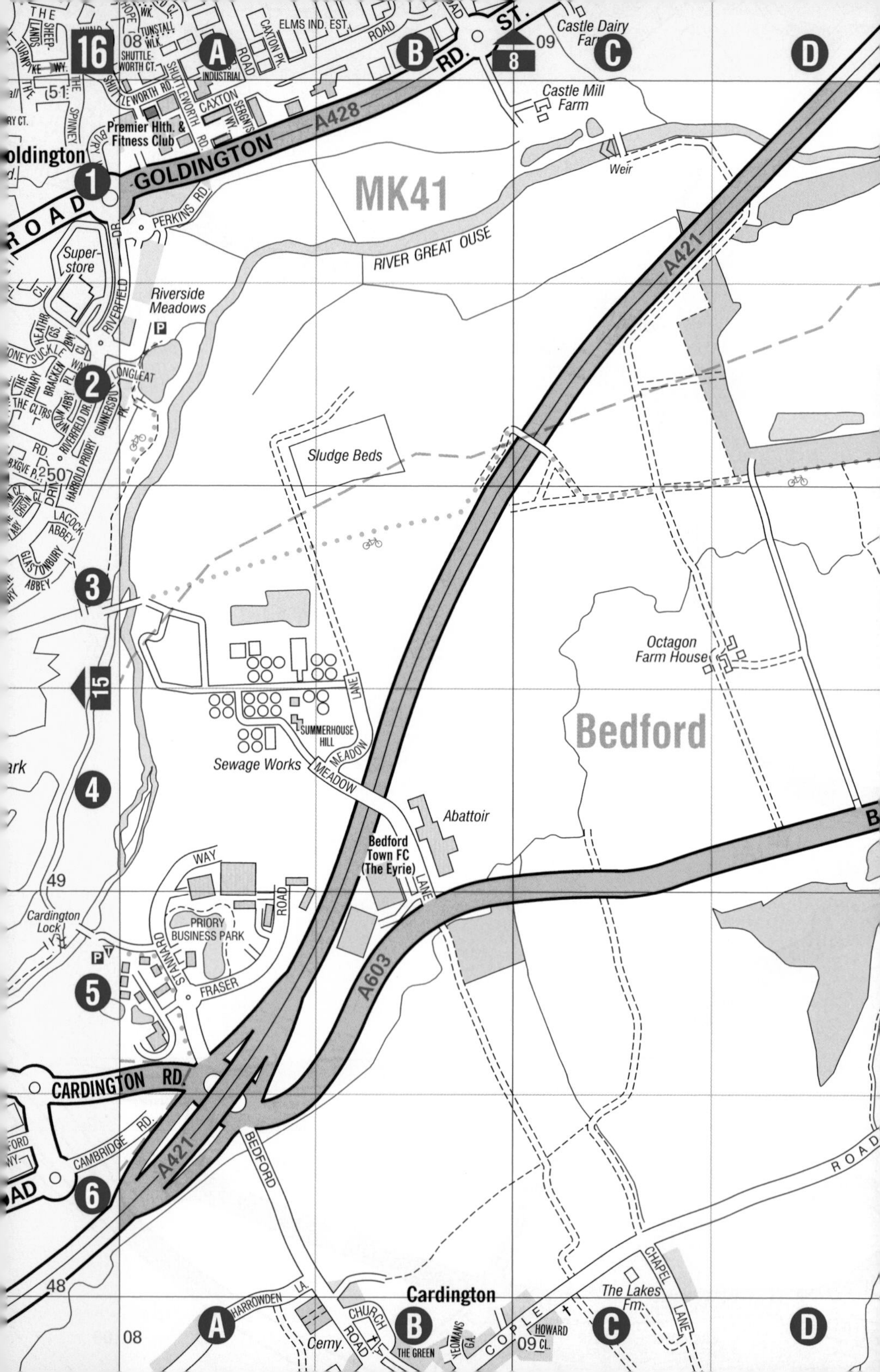

16
A
B
C
D
1
2
3
4
5
6
8
15
08
09
51
50
49
48
ELMS IND. EST.
Castle Dairy Farm
Castle Mill Farm
Premier Hlth. & Fitness Club
GOLDINGTON RD.
ST.
A428
Goldington
ROAD
Weir
MK41
RIVER GREAT OUSE
PERKINS RD.
Super-store
RIVERFIELD DR.
Riverside Meadows
LONGLEAT
GUNNERSBURY PK.
HARROLD PRIORY
LACOCK ABBEY
GLASTONBURY ABBEY
A421
Sludge Beds
Octagon Farm House
Bedford
SUMMERHOUSE HILL
Sewage Works
MEADOW LANE
Abattoir
Bedford Town FC (The Eyrie)
LANE
WAY
ROAD
PRIORY BUSINESS PARK
STANNARD
FRASER
Cardington Lock
A603
CARDINGTON RD.
CAMBRIDGE RD.
BEDFORD ROAD
ROAD
CHAPEL LANE
The Lakes Fm.
Cardington
HARROWDEN LA.
CHURCH ROAD
Cemy.
THE GREEN
YEOMANS GA.
COPLE
HOWARD CL.

E
F
9
11
G
H
12
Gadsey Brook Cottage
51
1
Willington Lock
RIVER GREAT OUSE
Riverside Vis. Cen.
Danish Camp
2
Nursery
Willington Lwr. Sch.
Play. Fld.
CHURCH
CHURCHILL PL.
ROAD
CHAPEL
LANE
MOWBRAY PL.
STATION
RUSSELL DR.
BEAUCHAMP PL.
ROAD
250
Dovecote & Stables
END CHURCH
CHURCH
BALLS
WILLINGTON
GOSTWICK PL.
BARFORD
Garden Centre
3
Riding Centre for the Handicapped
GRANGE WY.
ROAD
20
10
ROAD
SANDY
25
LANE
49
23
WOOD
39
38
42
18
RD.
A603
DFORD
4
WILLINGTON
Gravel Pit Spinney
MK44
ALL SAINTS RD.
RYE CRES.
49
Home Farm
ROTHER CT.
LANE
COPLE
5
Cople Lower Sch.
ROAD
BURRSHOLT
LANE
NORTHILL
Playing Field
6
WOODLANDS CL.
48
Water End
END
WATER
E
F
ROAD
11
G
H
12

**A**   **B**   **10**   13   **C**   **D**

**1**
51

Willington Lock

RIVER GREAT OUSE

ROAD

**2**
²50

BARFORD

Guy's Wood

Bedford
MK44

en Centre

**3**
25   39

MID BEDFORDSHIRE
BEDFORD

Willowhill
Farm

**17** **SANDY**   ROAD BEDFORD

A603   THE AVENUE   63   A60

**4**
49

WOOD

ROAD
PARK

PARK ROAD   PARK

Bottom
Wood

**5**

LANE WOOD

Hill Farm   Conduit Grove

Moggerhanger
Park

ST. JOHN'S

**6**

LANE

Grove Farm
House

BUDNA

Sheerhatch
Wood

48

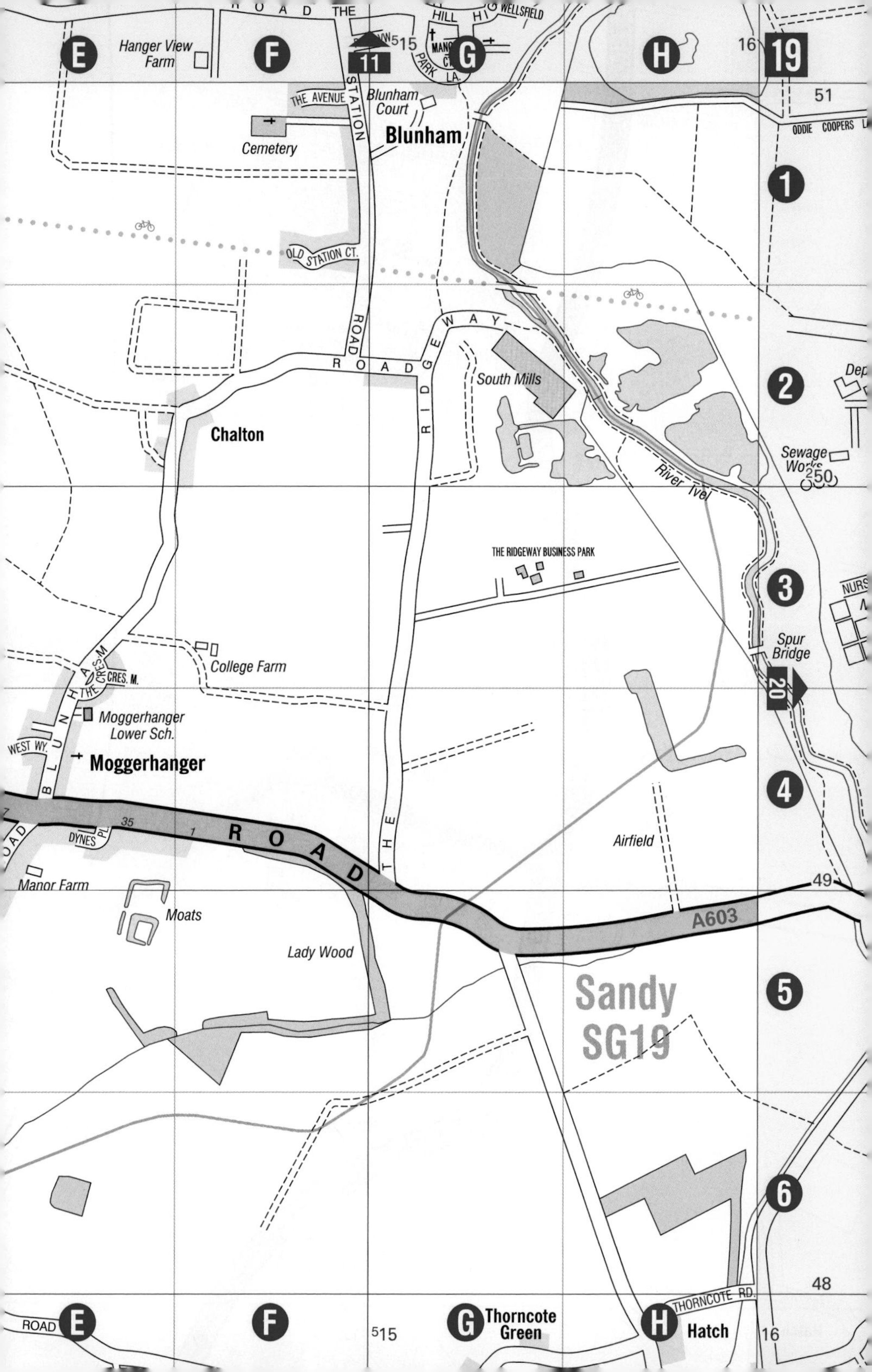

E
F
G
H
19
11
20
1
2
3
4
5
6
Hanger View Farm
THE AVENUE
STATION ROAD
Blunham Court
Blunham
Cemetery
PARK LA.
WELLSFIELD
HILL
16
51
ODDIE
COOPERS
OLD STATION CT.
RIDGEWAY
ROAD
THE RIDGEWAY
South Mills
Chalton
River Ivel
Sewage Works
50
THE RIDGEWAY BUSINESS PARK
Spur Bridge
College Farm
THE CRES.
CRES. M.
BLUNHAM
Moggerhanger Lower Sch.
WEST WY.
Moggerhanger
DYNES PL.
35
ROAD
Manor Farm
Moats
Airfield
49
A603
Lady Wood
Sandy SG19
48
THORNCOTE RD.
Thorncote Green
Hatch
515
16

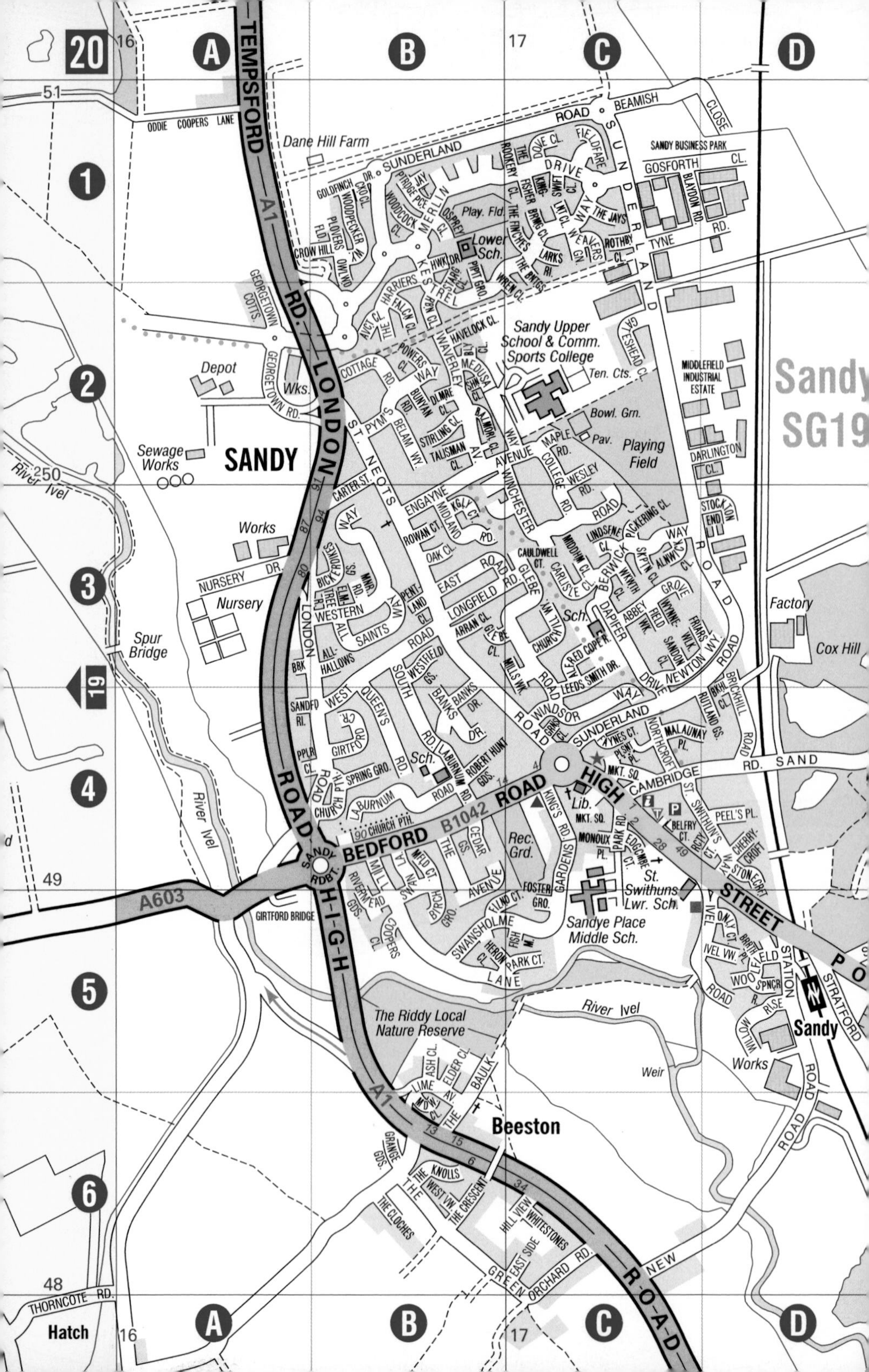

A
B
C
D
1
2
3
4
5
6
16
17
51
49
48
TEMPSFORD
A1
LONDON RD.
SANDY
Sandy SG19
ODDIE COOPERS LANE
Dane Hill Farm
SUNDERLAND ROAD
BEAMISH CLOSE
SANDY BUSINESS PARK
GOSFORTH CL.
BLAYDON RD.
TYNE RD.
ROTHBY CL.
MIDDLEFIELD INDUSTRIAL ESTATE
DARLINGTON CL.
STOCKTON END
Play. Fld.
Lower Sch.
Sandy Upper School & Comm. Sports College
Ten. Cts.
Bowl. Grn.
Pav.
Playing Field
GEORGETOWN COTTS.
GEORGETOWN RD.
Depot
Wks.
Sewage Works
River Ivel
Works
NURSERY DR.
Nursery
Spur Bridge
19
ST. NEOTS ROAD
CARTER ST.
ENGAYNE AV.
WINCHESTER RD.
MAPLE RD.
COLLEGE RD.
WESLEY RD.
PICKERING CL.
BERWICK WAY
CAULDWELL CT.
LONGFIELD RD.
EAST RD.
GLEBE RD.
Sch.
WESTERN WAY
ALL SAINTS
ALL-HALLOWS
WEST RD.
QUEEN'S GRO.
GIRTFORD CR.
SPRING GRO.
SOUTH RD.
WESTFIELD GS.
BANKS DR.
LABURNUM RD.
ROBERT HUNT GDS.
CHURCH PTH.
BEDFORD ROAD B1042
SANDY RDBT.
WINDSOR ROAD
SUNDERLAND RD.
HIGH STREET
MKT. SQ.
CAMBRIDGE RD.
SAND
Lib.
KING'S RD.
Rec. Grd.
CEDAR GS.
AVENUE
St. Swithuns Lwr. Sch.
Sandye Place Middle Sch.
Factory
Cox Hill
BRICKHILL ROAD
STATION ROAD
STRATFORD ROAD
Sandy
Works
A603
GIRTFORD BRIDGE
HIGH ROAD
The Riddy Local Nature Reserve
River Ivel
Weir
Beeston
THE BAULK
GRANGE GDS.
THE KNOLLS
THE CRESCENT
WEST VW.
THE CLOCHES
HILL VIEW
WHITESTONES
EAST SIDE
GREEN
ORCHARD RD.
NEW ROAD
THORNCOTE RD.
Hatch

21
E
F
G
H
19
520
Everton
51
Recre
Grou
1
2
3
4
5
6
250
49
48
22
ROAD
SANDY
ROAD
Lowfield Farm
The Rookery
Hazells Hall
Hazells Hall Fm.
Park Plantation
Lord's Wood
Sandy Heath
LONG RIDING
LANE
EVERTON
SWADEN
Quarry Hills
Camp
Swading Hill
Reservoir (Covered)
ROAD
B1042
etery
Visitor Centre
Redstone Hill
The Lodge Nature Reserve (RSPB)
Sandy Warren
Bunker's Hill
The Lodge
ROAD

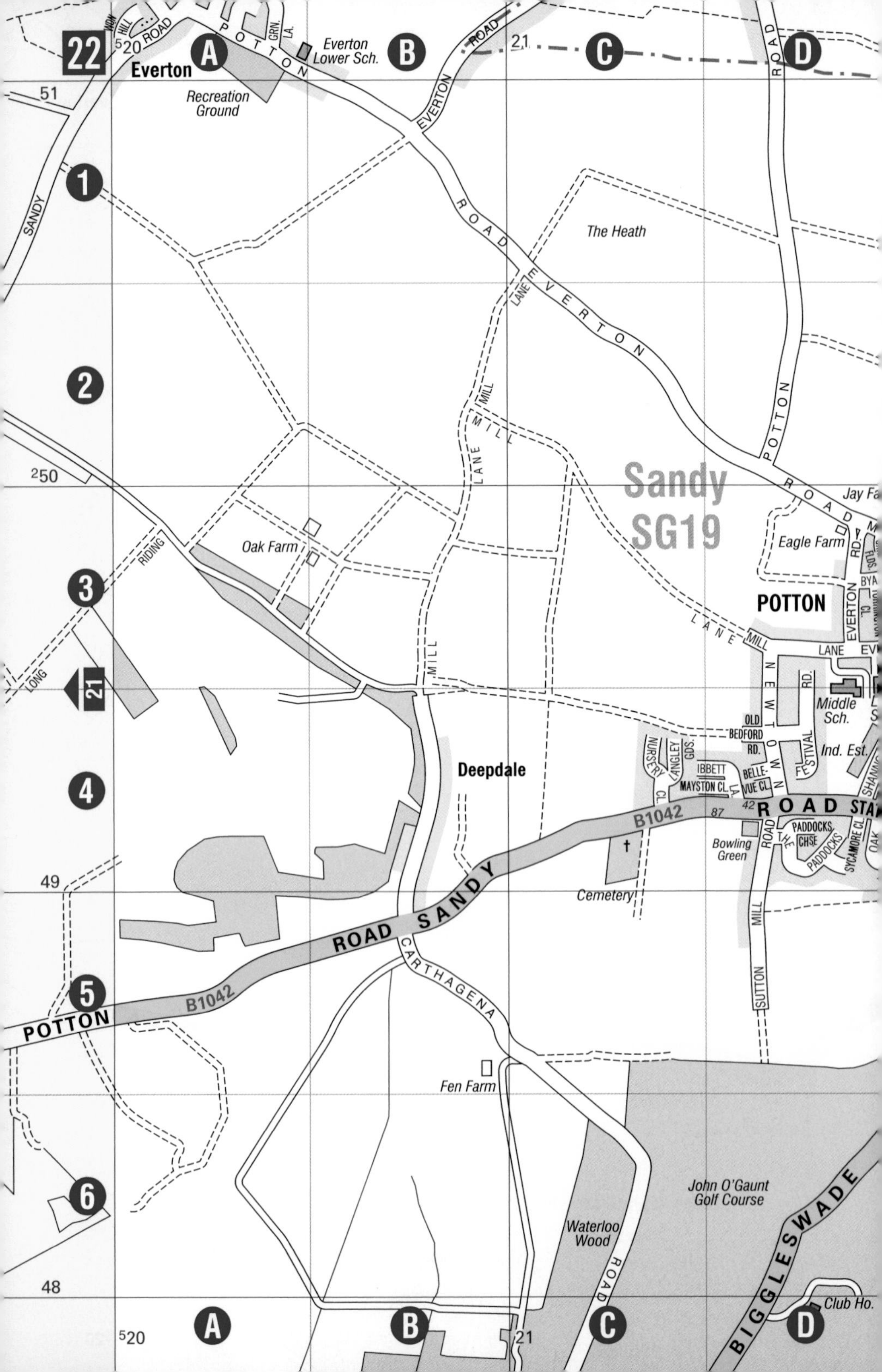
22
Everton
Everton Lower Sch.
Recreation Ground
POTTON ROAD
EVERTON ROAD
SANDY
The Heath
EVERTON ROAD
LANE
MILL LANE
POTTON ROAD
Sandy SG19
Jay Fa
Eagle Farm
POTTON
Oak Farm
RIDING
LONG
21
MILL LANE
Middle Sch.
Ind. Est.
OLD BEDFORD RD.
NURSERY CL.
LANGLEY GDS.
IBBETT
MAYSTON CL.
BELLE-VUE CL.
NEWTOWN
FESTIVAL
Deepdale
B1042
SANDY ROAD
Bowling Green
Cemetery
MILL
SUTTON ROAD
THE PADDOCKS
SYCAMORE CL.
POTTON
CARTHAGENA
Fen Farm
John O'Gaunt Golf Course
Waterloo Wood
ROAD
BIGGLESWADE
Club Ho.
A
B
C
D
1
2
3
4
5
6
51
250
49
48
520
21

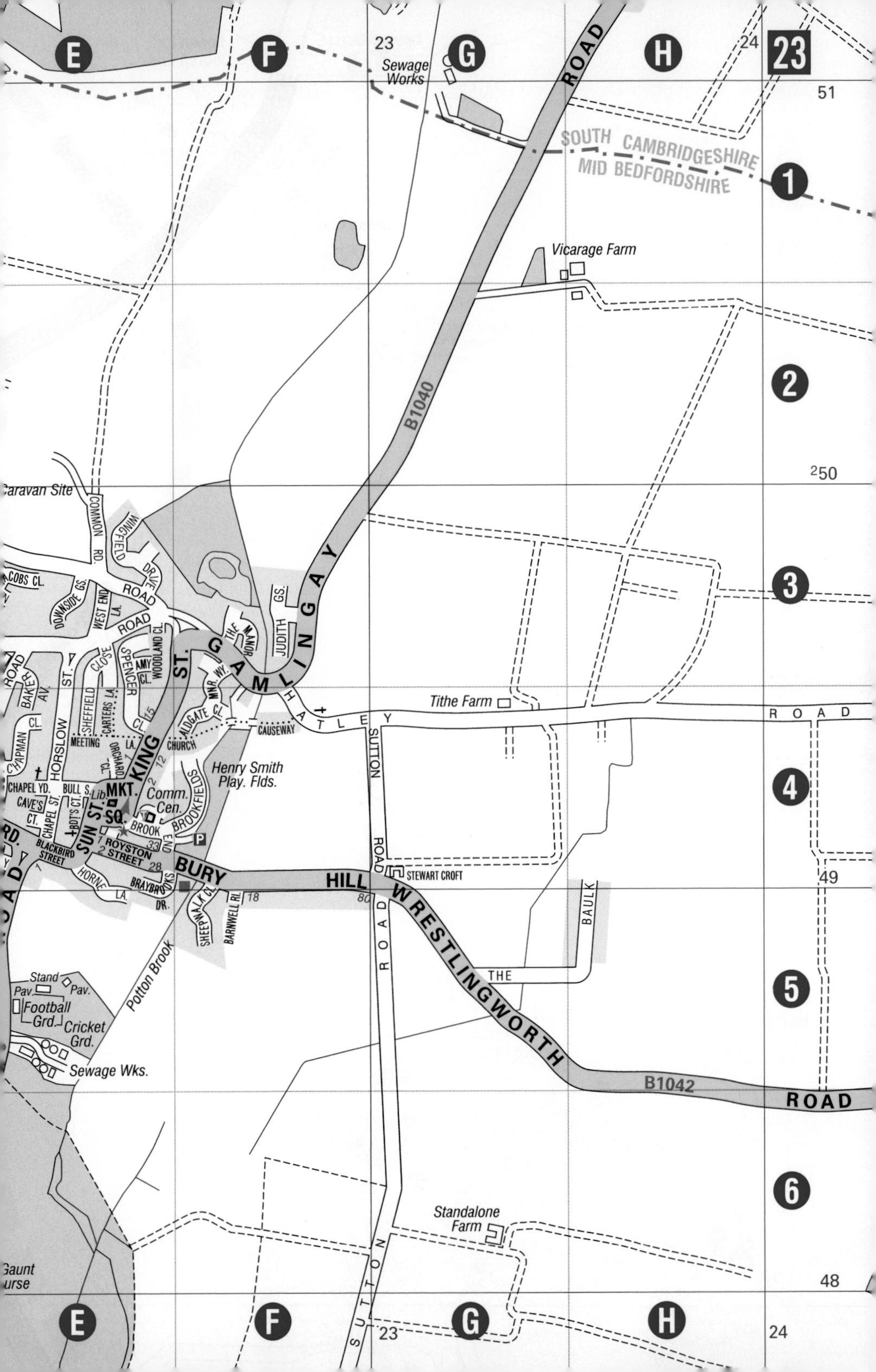

23
E
F
G
H
1
2
3
4
5
6
Sewage Works
ROAD
SOUTH CAMBRIDGESHIRE
MID BEDFORDSHIRE
Vicarage Farm
B1040
Caravan Site
COMMON RD.
WINGFIELD DRIVE
ROAD
GAMLINGAY
JUDITH GS.
THE MANOR
WOODLAND CL.
AMY CL.
SPENCER CL.
KING ST.
MKT. SQ.
SUN ST.
HATLEY ROAD
CAUSEWAY
Tithe Farm
SUTTON ROAD
Henry Smith Play. Flds.
Comm. Cen.
BROOKFIELDS
BROOK END
ROYSTON STREET
BLACKBIRD STREET
BURY HILL
STEWART CROFT
WRESTLINGWORTH ROAD
B1042
THE BAULK
HORNE LA.
BRAYBROOKS DR.
SHEEPWALK CL.
BARNWELL RI.
Potton Brook
Football Grd.
Cricket Grd.
Sewage Wks.
Standalone Farm
SUTTON
24
51
250
49
48

**24**

48

47

46

245

500

**A** **B** **C** **D**

Vicarage 01
12

Kempston
Church End
Weir

Box End Rd. Cemetery

A5134

River

(Proposed)

(Proposed)

Glenbrook
Farm

Tithe

1

Green End

Cemetery

Road

End

Play.
Fld.
P
Church
Rd.
Hall

Kempston
Rural Lwr. Sch.

2

Kempston House

Old
Grooms
Cott.

Rose Cottage

Green

Home

Road

The Bury

Hill

The Dell

Tythe Farm

Ibbett Cl.

Cl.

The
Chase

Ridge

3

Road
Wood
End
Lane
Road

Brook
Farm

Wood End
Farm

Wood End Road

Bell Farm

MK43

4

Keeley Hall

Tinker's
Corner

Lane End Road

Bedford Rd.
Wootton

Keeley Farm

5

**Hall End**

Hall End
Farm

End

**WOOTTON**

Cemetery

Canons Cl.

Mepham

Neale

Thorpe

Foster Rd. Way

Walk

Halegate

Rec.
Grd.

The
Cedars

Elmsdale

Walnut
Rd.
Oak Cl.

Cross

The
Willows

Stables
Ct.

Potters

Manor Rd.

Pav.

Football
Ground

Lib.

Farm
Rd.

Hanover Ct.

Road

6

Studley Rd.

Lorraine

Popes
Wy.

Road

St. Marys Rd.

Barn
Rd.

Wootton
Lwr. Sch.

Rec. Grd.

Bedford

Fields

Grovebury
Ct.

Beauchamp

Payne

Cynla

Church

Cause

St. Marys

Tithe

Old Sch. La.

Road

Road

Wootton
Upper
School

Tennis Cts.

Ch. Rw.

Cerny

Russell Way

01

Wootton
Wood

500
Play. Fld.

**A** **B** **C** **D**

25
13
26
KEMPSTON
Bedford
MK40
MK42
MK45
OUSE
HIGH STREET
BEDFORD ROAD
ST. JOHN'S ST.
WOBURN ROAD
A5134
A421
B531
B530
AMPTHILL RD.
AMPTHILL ROAD
BEDFORD HARDWICK HILL AMPTHILL RD.
ELSTOW ROAD
CHANTRY AVENUE
CHANTRY ROAD
ORCHARD
HIGHFIELD RD.
SPRINGFIELD AV.
Robert Bruce Middle Sch.
Camestone Lower Sch.
Daubeney Middle Sch.
Springfield Lwr. Sch.
Balliol Lwr. Sch.
Hastingsbury Upper Sch. & Comm. Coll.
Police HQ
Sports Ground
Sports Fld.
Superstore
SAXON CENTRE
ST. JOHN'S HOMES
INTERCHANGE RETAIL PARK
WOBURN ROAD INDUSTRIAL ESTATE
WOBURN RD. IND. EST.
WOLSELEY BUS. PK.
MARSH LEYS
Stanley Works
Elms Farm
Hardwick Bridge
Kempston Hardwick
Kempston Hardwick Crossing
Works
Yth. Cen.
Playground
School
Lwr. Sch.
Tennis Cts.
Bowl. Grn.
Ten. Cts.
Bowls
MANOR ROAD
E
F
G
H
1
2
3
4
5
6
03
04
245
46
47
48

26
A
B
C
D
14
South End
Works
Pioneer Park
Play Area
MILE
A5134
AMPTHILL
A421
PROGRESS WY.
WEST END
RD.
A6
MK42
Elstow Moot Hall
Remains of Abbey
Elstow Lower Sch.
Abbey Middle School
ELSTOW
Playground
Elstow Lwr. Sch.
Elstow Play. Fld.
Pav.
P+R Elstow
PROGRESS PARK
Pear Tree Farm
Factory
Works
Springfield Lwr. Sch.
Ten. Cts
INTERCHANGE RETAIL PARK
RACE MEADOWS
25
AMPTHILL ROAD
B530
REFUSE TIP
Recycling Centre
WILSTEAD RD.
BEDFORD RD.
MK45
HARDWICK HILL
28
WATSON RD.
1
2
3
4
5
6
48
47
46
45
04
505
Ind. Est.
Mill
Abbey Fields
MEDBURY LA.
PEAR TREE ROAD
LYNN CL.
MOSS LANE
SOUTH AVENUE
WILSTEAD
ROMSEY WY.
TITCHFIELD DR.
CROXDEN WY.
TEWKESBURY R.
MELROSE DR.
WALTHAM DR.
BAYHAM
MOWBRAY WAY
BERKELEY ROAD
GOSTWICK RD.
BLUNDELL PL.
MOOR
CORBY CL.
STAPLETON R.
WINDSOR
MILE ROAD
BRACKLEY
GLOUCESTER
HAREWOOD
LANCASTER
KENT
BROAD
ELSTOW ROAD

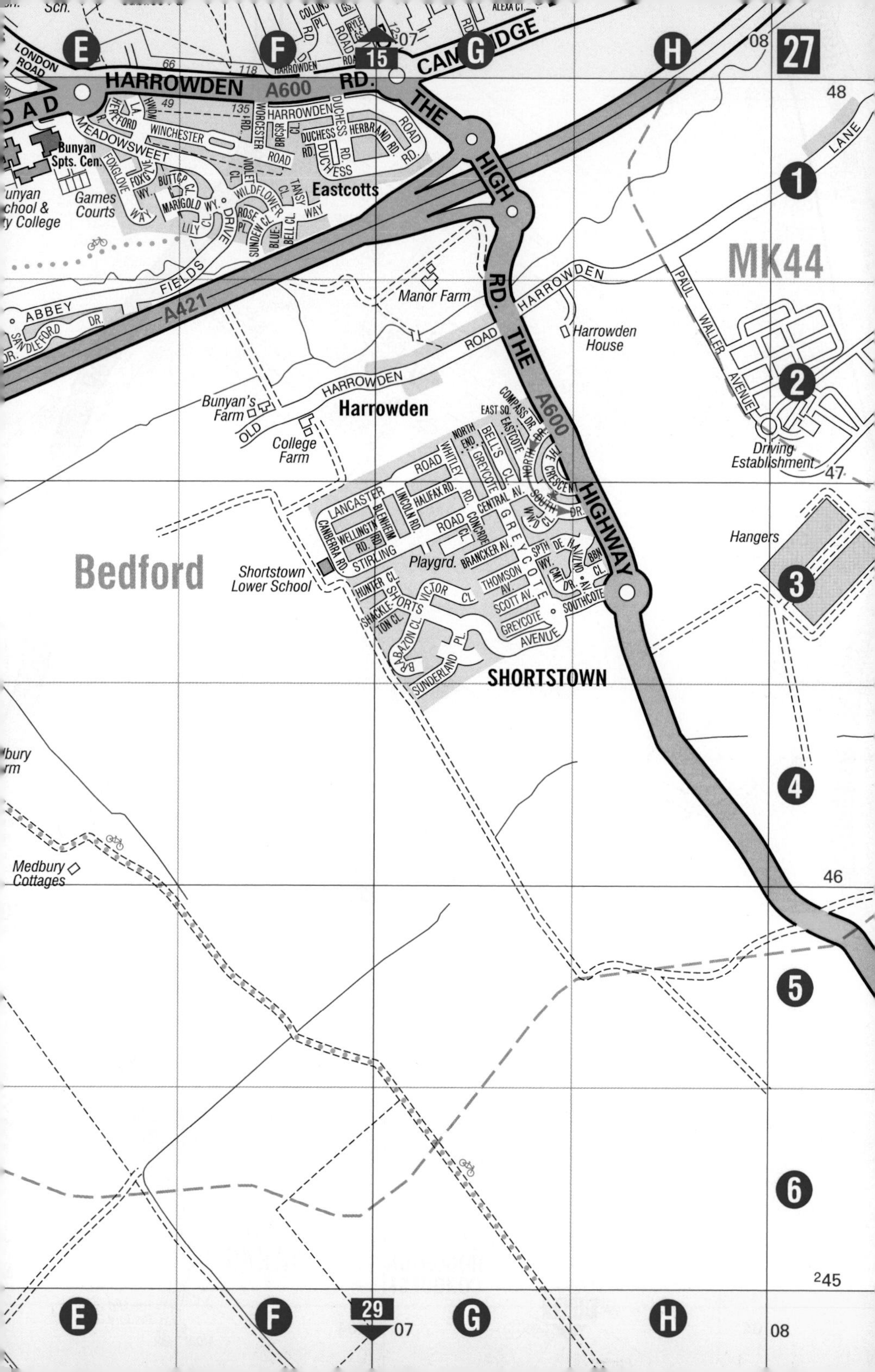

E
F
G
H
15
07
08
48
47
46
45
1
2
3
4
5
6
HARROWDEN RD.
A600
CAMBRIDGE
LONDON ROAD
ROAD
Bunyan Spts. Cen.
Bunyan School &
Games Courts
Eastcotts
MEADOWSWEET
WINCHESTER
HEREFORD
FOXGLOVE WAY
MARIGOLD WY.
LILY CL.
DRIVE
ROSE PL.
SUNDEW CL.
BLUE-BELL CL.
TANSY WAY
WILDFLOWER
VIOLET CL.
WORCESTER ROAD
HARROWDEN CL.
DUCHESS RD.
HERBRAND RD.
THE HIGH RD.
A421
FIELDS
ABBEY
SANDLEFORD DR.
MK44
LANE
PAUL WALLER AVENUE
Driving Establishment
Manor Farm
HARROWDEN ROAD
Harrowden House
OLD HARROWDEN
Bunyan's Farm
Harrowden
College Farm
THE HIGHWAY
Hangers
Bedford
Shortstown Lower School
LANCASTER
WELLINGTON
BLENHEIM RD.
LINCOLN RD.
HALIFAX RD.
WHITLEY RD.
BELL'S CL.
GREYCOTE
NORTH END
EASTCOTE
EAST SQ.
COMPASS DR.
THE CRESCENT
CENTRAL AV.
CONCORDE CL.
STIRLING
CANBERRA RD.
Playgrd.
BRANCKER AV.
DE HAVILAND AV.
THOMSON AV.
SCOTT AV.
HUNTER CL.
SHORTS
SHACKLETON CL.
VICTOR CL.
BRABAZON CL.
SUNDERLAND PL.
GREYCOTE AVENUE
SOUTHCOTE
SHORTSTOWN
Medbury Cottages
29

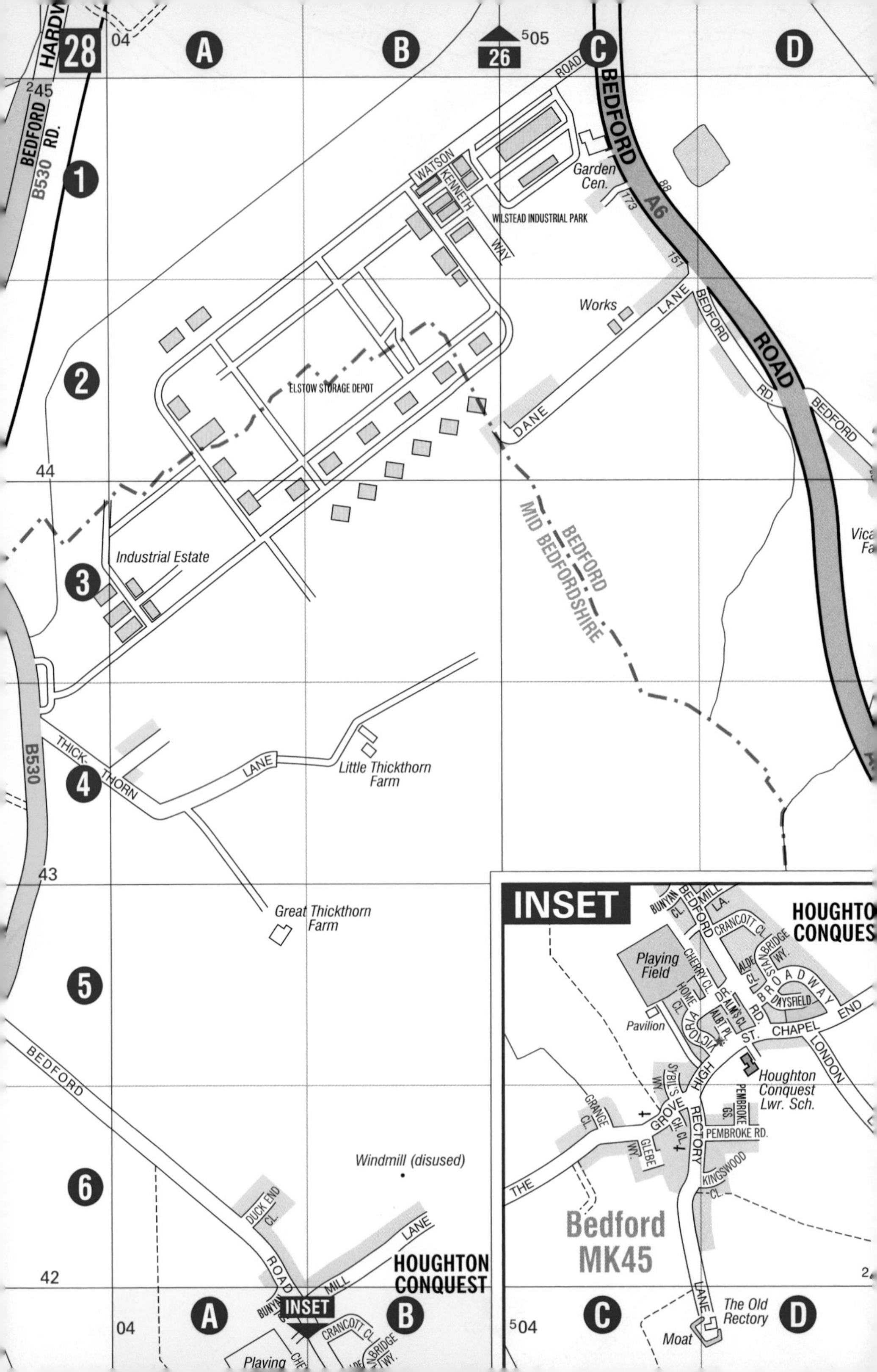

# 28

A · B · C · D

**1**

HARDW
BEDFORD RD.
B530
245
04
505
▲ 26
BEDFORD A6
ROAD

Garden Cen.

WATSON
KENNETH WAY
WILSTEAD INDUSTRIAL PARK

88
173
151

Works

BEDFORD RD.

LANE

BEDFORD RD.

BEDFORD

**2**

ELSTOW STORAGE DEPOT

44

DANE

BEDFORD MID BEDFORDSHIRE

Vica
Fa

**3**

Industrial Estate

**4**

B530
THICK-THORN
LANE
Little Thickthorn Farm

43

**5**

BEDFORD

Great Thickthorn Farm

**6**

42

Windmill (disused)

DUCK END CL.

MILL LANE

BUNYAN ROAD

HOUGHTON CONQUEST

04

A · **INSET** · B · 504 · C · D

Playing

## INSET

BUNYAN CL.
BEDFORD
MILL LA.
CRANCOTT CL.
STANBRIDGE HWY.

HOUGHTON CONQUES

Playing Field

CHERRY CL.
HOME CL.
DR. ALINS CL.
VICTORIA PL.
MOAT PL.
DAYSFIELD RD.

BROADWAY

Pavilion

CHAPEL END

LONDON END

HIGH ST.

SYBIL'S WY.
GROVE CH. CL.
GLEBE WY.

RECTORY

PEMBROKE RD.
PEMBROKE GS.

Houghton Conquest Lwr. Sch.

GRANGE CL.
THE

KINGSWOOD CL.

**Bedford MK45**

LANE

The Old Rectory

Moat

C · D

2

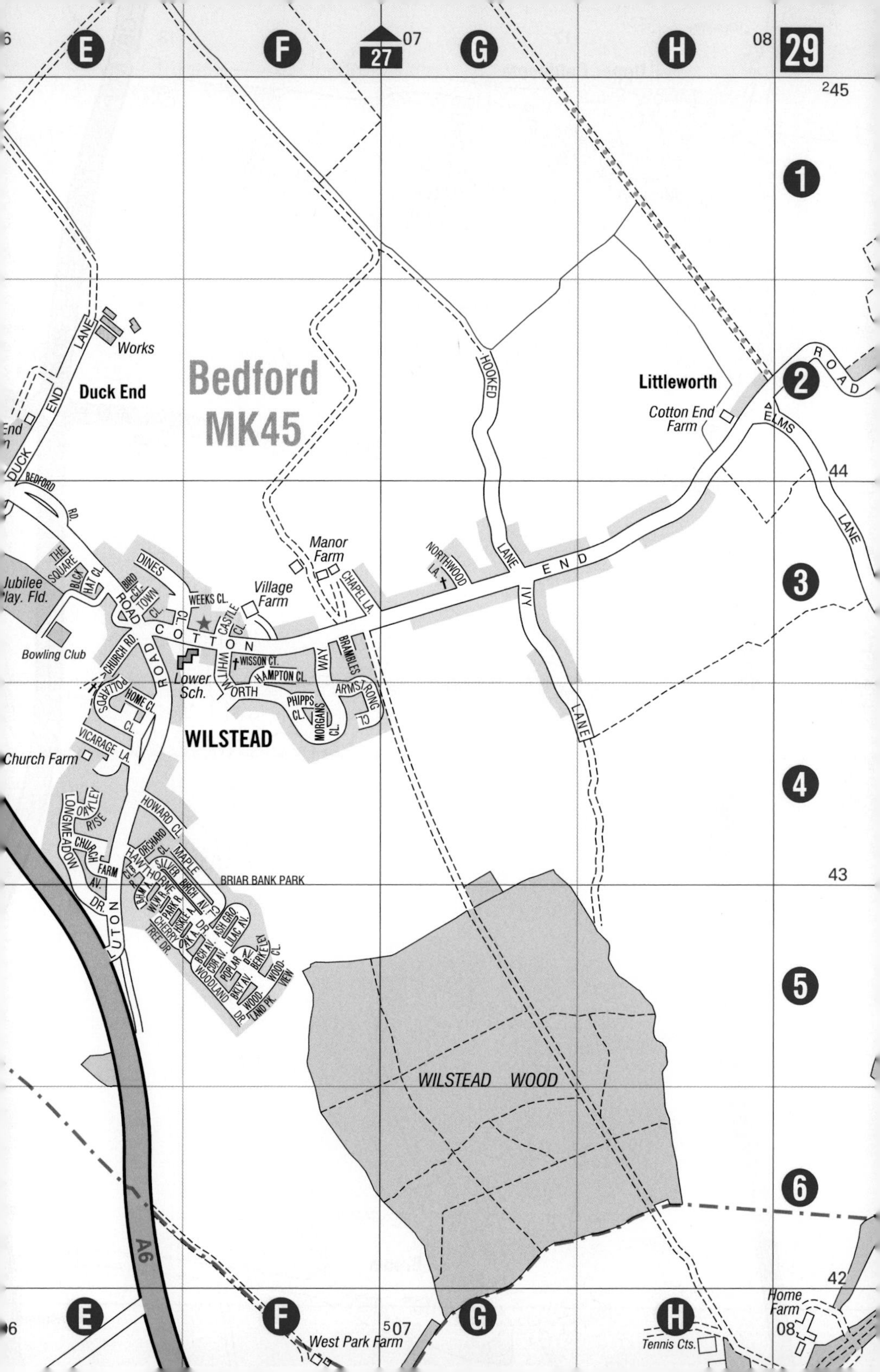
E
F
G
H
27
07
08
245
44
43
42
1
2
3
4
5
6
Bedford
MK45
Duck End
Works
DUCK END LANE
Littleworth
Cotton End Farm
ELMS LANE
ROAD
HOOKED LANE
Manor Farm
Village Farm
NORTHWOOD LA.
CHAPEL LA.
COTTON END
IVY LANE
BEDFORD RD.
THE SQUARE
BLCK HAT CL.
BIRD CL.
DINES
TOWN CL.
WEEKS CL.
CASTLE CL.
Jubilee Play. Fld.
Bowling Club
CHURCH RD.
COTTON ROAD
Lower Sch.
WHITWORTH
WISSON CT.
HAMPTON CL.
WAY
BRAMBLES
ARMSTRONG CL.
PHIPPS CL.
MORGANS CL.
POLLARDS
HOME CL.
CL.
WILSTEAD
VICARAGE LA.
Church Farm
OAKLEY RISE
LONGMEADOW
CHURCH FARM AV.
HOWARD CL.
ORCHARD CL.
MAPLE
HAWTHORNE
SILVER BIRCH AV.
BRIAR BANK PARK
LUTON DR.
CHERRY TREE DR.
ASH GRO.
LILAC AV.
BERKELEY CL.
POPLAR AV.
WOODLAND DR.
WOOD-VIEW
WOODLAND PK.
WILSTEAD WOOD
A6
West Park Farm
Tennis Cts.
Home Farm
507
08

**30**

46

Cemetery

**A**

17

**B**

**C**

18

**D**

**Upper Caldecote**

SWALLOW FIELD

ROAD

Tingey's Corner

Elmco

ICKWELL RD.

BIGGLESWADE ROAD

POUND CL.

OAK CR.

HITCHIN ROAD

**1**

MNR. CT.

MANOR PL.

DENE

WAY

ASHBY CL.

BROOK CL.

SHAKESPEARE DR.

BYRON CL.

NORTH DR.

WORDS

HARVEY CL.

THE PASTURES

NORTH-A1 ROAD

BELLS

Supers

Caldecote Lwr. Sch.

Waterlane Fm.

Pavs.

Play. Fld.

Woodlands Nurseries

CALDECOTE GREEN

**2**

245

Depot

HILL

**HILL**

**LANE**

B658

Driving Range

HILL LANE CROSSROADS

HILL LANE CROSSROADS

B658

**3**

Sand and Gravel Pit

LANE

The Hill House

The Moat Cottage

**Biggleswade**

**4**

44

**SG18**

**5**

**6**

KING'S RD

HIGH

ROAD

GYPSY

Facto

THE MAYNARDS

STREET

HIGH

THE WOODLANDS

**Broom**

BROOM HALL

43

B658

**A**

BANCROFT AV.

HIGH

**B**

SOUTHILL

**C**

18

**D** Holme

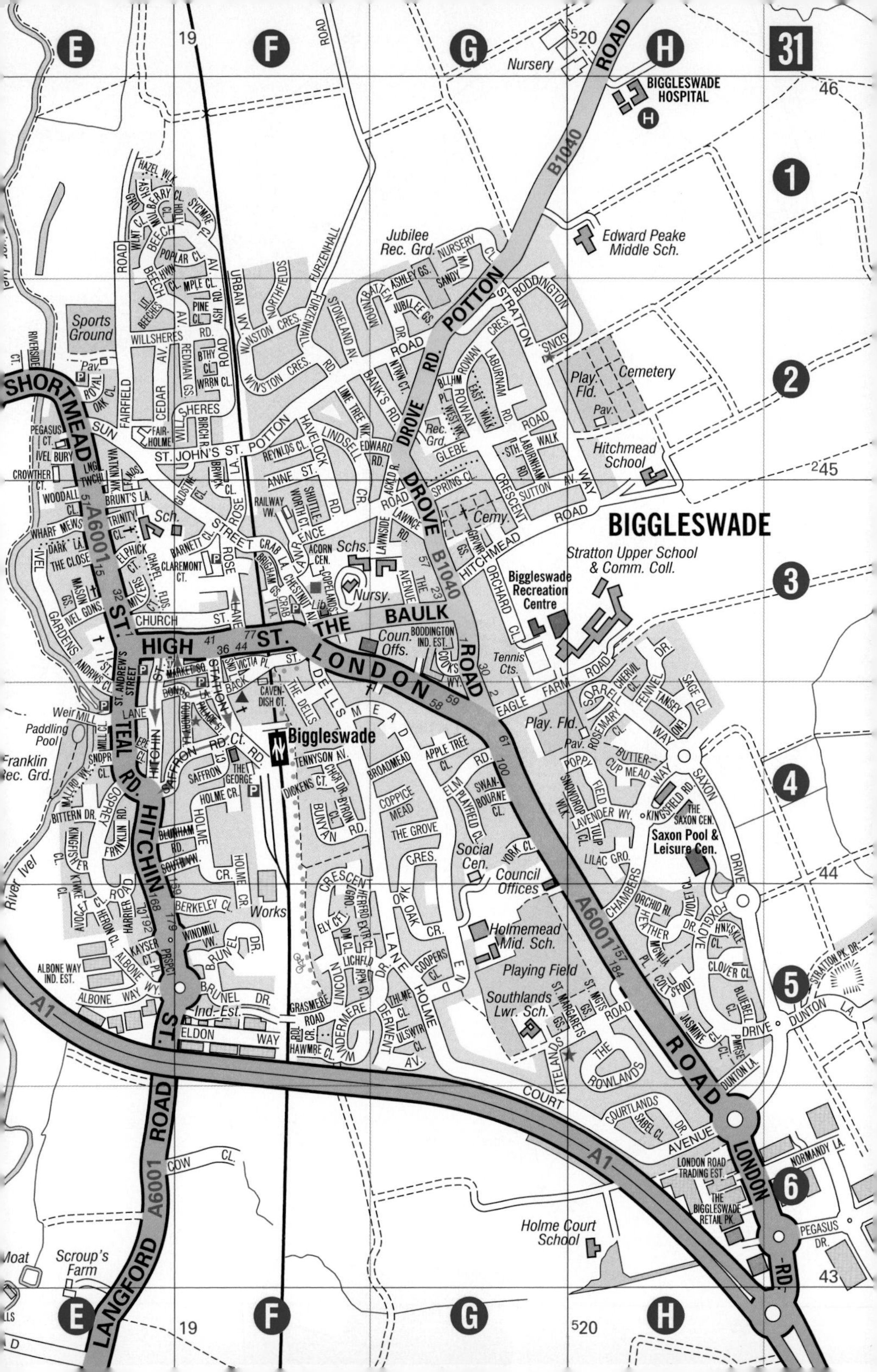

E
F
G
H
19
520
46
45
44
43
1
2
3
4
5
6
BIGGLESWADE
BIGGLESWADE HOSPITAL
Nursery
Edward Peake Middle Sch.
Jubilee Rec. Grd.
Sports Ground
Cemetery
Play. Fld.
Pav.
Hitchmead School
Stratton Upper School & Comm. Coll.
Biggleswade Recreation Centre
Tennis Cts.
Coun. Offs.
Biggleswade
Social Cen.
Council Offices
Holmemead Mid. Sch.
Playing Field
Southlands Lwr. Sch.
Saxon Pool & Leisure Cen.
THE SAXON CEN.
Works
Holme Court School
Scroup's Farm
Moat
Paddling Pool
Franklin Rec. Grd.
River Ivel
Weir
Cemy.
Nursy.
Schs.
Sch.
Lib.
Rec. Grd.
ALBONE WAY IND. EST.
LONDON ROAD TRADING EST.
THE BIGGLESWADE RETAIL PK.
BODDINGTON IND. EST.
Ind. Est.
SHORTMEAD ST.
HIGH ST.
LONDON ROAD
THE BAULK
DROVE RD.
POTTON ROAD
HITCHIN ST.
LANGFORD ROAD
TEAL RD.
A6001
B1040
A1
ST. JOHN'S ST.
CHURCH ST.
SUN ST.
STATION RD.
SAFFRON RD.
HOLME CR.
HOLME CT.
BRUNEL DR.
ALBONE WAY
ELDON WAY
EAGLE FARM ROAD
SAXON DRIVE
DUNTON LA.
STRATTON PK. DR.
COURT AVENUE
NORMANDY LA.
PEGASUS DR.
COW CL.
HITCHMEAD ROAD
LAUREL WALK
BODDINGTON
STRATTON WAY
ORCHARD CL.
GLEBE ROAD
SPRING CL.
WINSTON CRES.
FURZENHALL RD.
STONELAND AV.
MOUNTBATTEN DR.
JUBILEE GS.
ASHLEY GS.
NURSERY CL.
SANDY WAY
URBAN WY.
NORTHFIELDS
WILLSHERES RD.
FAIRFIELD
CEDAR AV.
REDMAN GS.
ROSE LA.
CRAB LA.
CHESTNUT AV.
LAWRENCE ROAD
LAWNSIDE
ACORN CEN.
THE AVENUE
DELLS MEAD
THE DELLS
TENNYSON AV.
DICKENS CT.
BROADMEAD
COPPICE MEAD
THE GROVE
APPLE TREE CL.
ELM RD.
PLAYFIELD CL.
SWANBOURNE CL.
YORK CL.
OAK CR.
COOPERS CL.
HOLME LANE END
DERWENT AV.
GRASMERE ROAD
WINDERMERE
LINCOLN
BUNYAN RD.
KITELANDS
ST. MARGARETS
THE ROWLANDS
COURTLANDS
SABEL CL.
CHAMBERS WAY
LILAC GRO.
LAVENDER WY.
POPPY FIELD
ROSEMARY CL.
SORRELL CL.
FENNEL WAY
TANSEY END
SAGE CL.
BUTTERCUP MEAD
KINGSHELD RD.
ORCHID RI.
HEATHER PL.
FOXGLOVE
CLOVER CL.
BLUEBELL CL.
JASMINE CL.
COLTSFOOT
VIOLET CL.
BITTERN DR.
OSPREY ROAD
FRANKLIN RD.
KINGFISHER CL.
HERON CL.
HARRIER CL.
MILL LANE
ST. ANDREW'S STREET
THE CLOSE
WHARF MEWS
WOODALL CL.
CROWTHER CT.
IVEL BURY
PEGASUS CT.
ROYAL OAK CL.
RIVERSIDE CT.
IVEL GARDENS
CLAREMONT CT.
BARNETT CL.
MARKET SQ.
CAVENDISH CT.
THE GEORGE
BLUNHAM RD.
SOUTH VW.
BERKELEY CL.
WINDMILL VW.
KAYSER CT.
HAZEL WLK
BEECH AV.
POPLAR CL.
PINE CL.
ASH RD.
BIRCH R.
EDWARD RD.
LINDSELL CR.
HAVELOCK RD.
ANNE ST.
RAILWAY VW.
LIME TREE WK.
BANK'S RD.
ROWAN CRES.
LABURNAM RD.
EAST WALK
WEST WK.
SUTTON AV.
CRESCENT

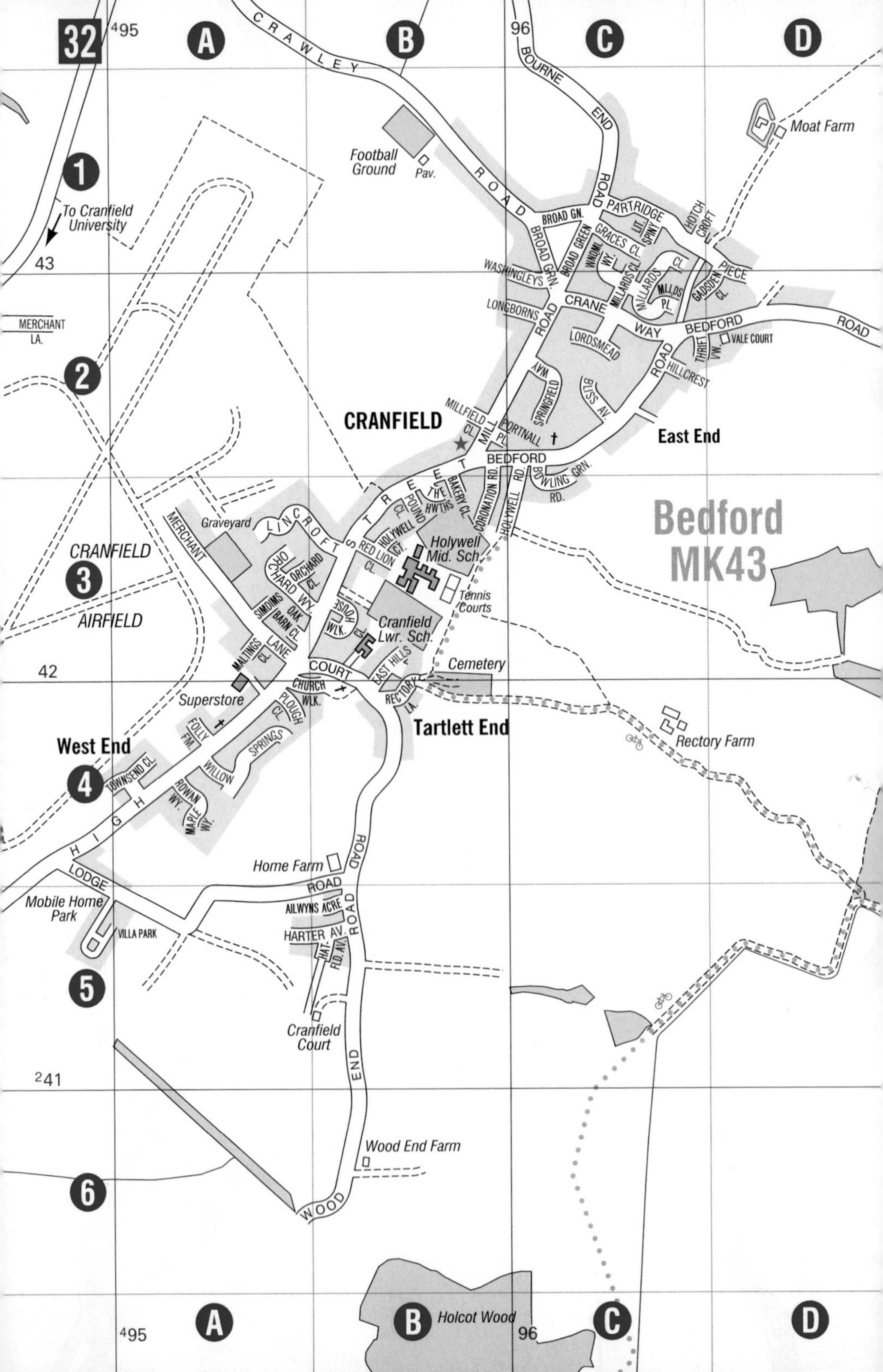

**32** 495

A    B    96    C    D

CRAWLEY

BOURNE END

ROAD

Moat Farm

**1**

To Cranfield
University

43

Football
Ground    Pav.

ROAD

BROAD GN.

PARTRIDGE

LITCH CROFT

BROAD GREEN

BROAD GRN.

GRACES CL.

CL.

WIDOW WY.

MILLARDS CL.

MILLARDS

PL.

GADSDEN

CL.

PIECE

MERCHANT
LA.

WASHINGLEYS

LONGBORNS

CRANE

WAY

BEDFORD

ROAD

**2**

LORDSMEAD

CRANE

ROAD

LORDSMEAD

WAY

SPRINGFIELD

WAY

BLISS AV.

HILLCREST

THRIFT

VW.

VALE COURT

**CRANFIELD**

MILLFIELD CL.

MILL PL.

PORTNALL

★

BEDFORD

**East End**

**Bedford
MK43**

CRANFIELD

Graveyard

LINCROFT

S T R E E T

POUND

HOLYWELL CL.

THE HWTHS.

BAKERY CL.

CORONATION RD.

HOLYWELL RD.

HOLYWELL

BOWLING GRN.

BOWLING
RD.

**3**

MERCHANT

ORCHARD WY.

ORCHARD CL.

RED LION CL.

Holywell
Mid. Sch.

AIRFIELD

SIMONDS WY.

OAK

BARN CL.

PINES WLK.

Cranfield
Lwr. Sch.

Tennis
Courts

42

MALTINGS CL.

LANE

COURT
WLK.

EAST HILLS

Cemetery

RECTORY

Superstore

CHURCH

WLK.

PLOUGH

RECTORY LA.

Rectory Farm

**West End**

SPRINGS

**Tartlett End**

FOLLY FM.

WILLOW

**4**

TOWNSEND CL.

HIGH

ROWAN WY.

MAPLE WY.

LODGE

Home Farm

ROAD

Mobile Home
Park

VILLA PARK

AILWYNS ACRE

HARTER AV.

NAT. RD. AV.

ROAD

**5**

Cranfield
Court

END

²41

Wood End Farm

**6**

WOOD

495    A    B    96    C    D

Holcot Wood

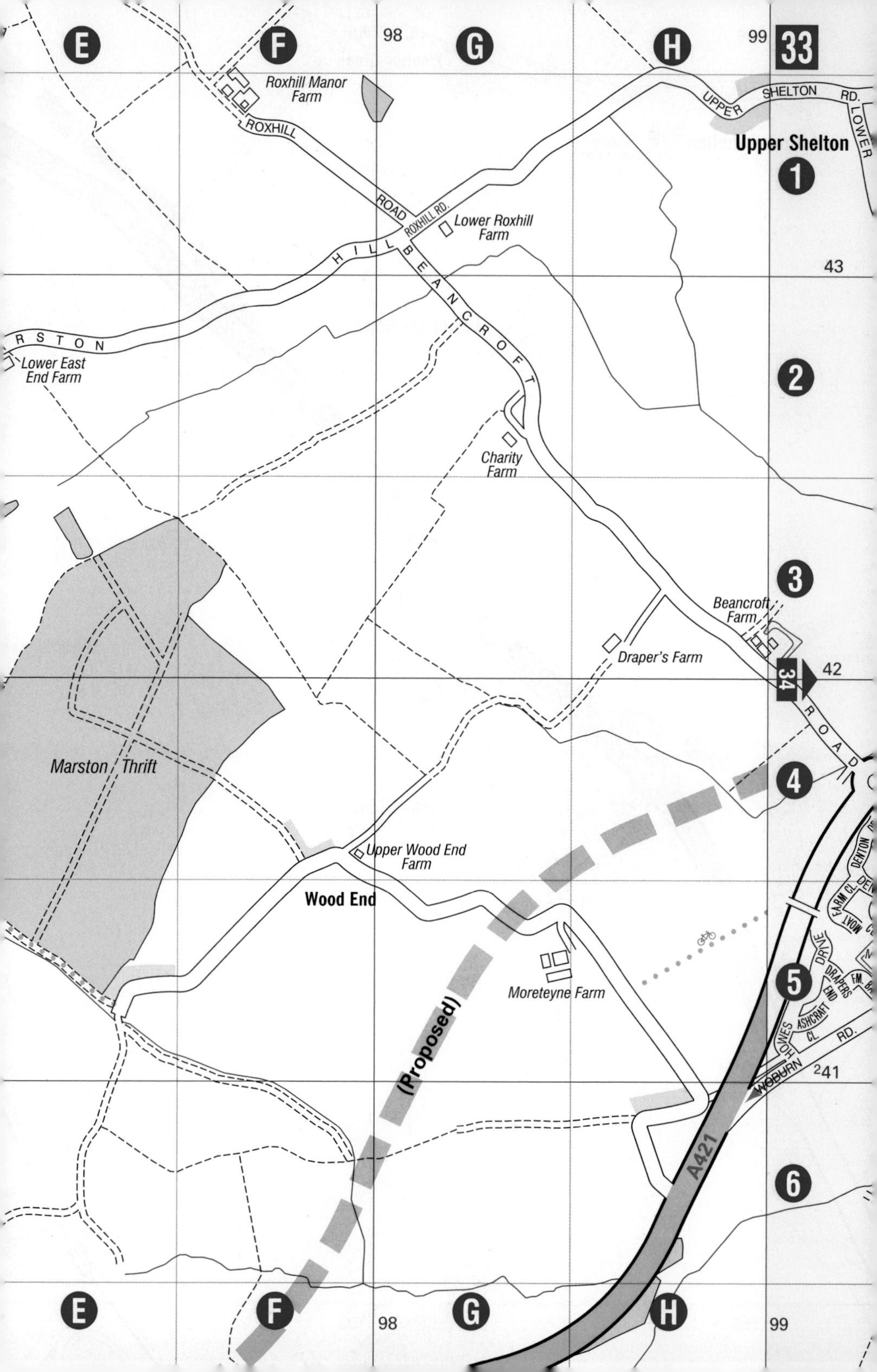

Roxhill Manor
Farm

ROXHILL

Upper Shelton

UPPER SHELTON RD. LOWER

ROAD

ROXHILL RD.

Lower Roxhill
Farm

HILL BEANCROFT

RSTON

Lower East
End Farm

Charity
Farm

Beancroft
Farm

Draper's Farm

**34** 42

ROAD

Marston Thrift

Upper Wood End
Farm

**Wood End**

MONKTON DEN

FARM CL.

MOAT

DRAPERS END

FM BA

(Proposed)

DRIVE

**5**

Moreteyne Farm

WOBURN

JONES ASHCRAFT
CL. RD.

241

A421

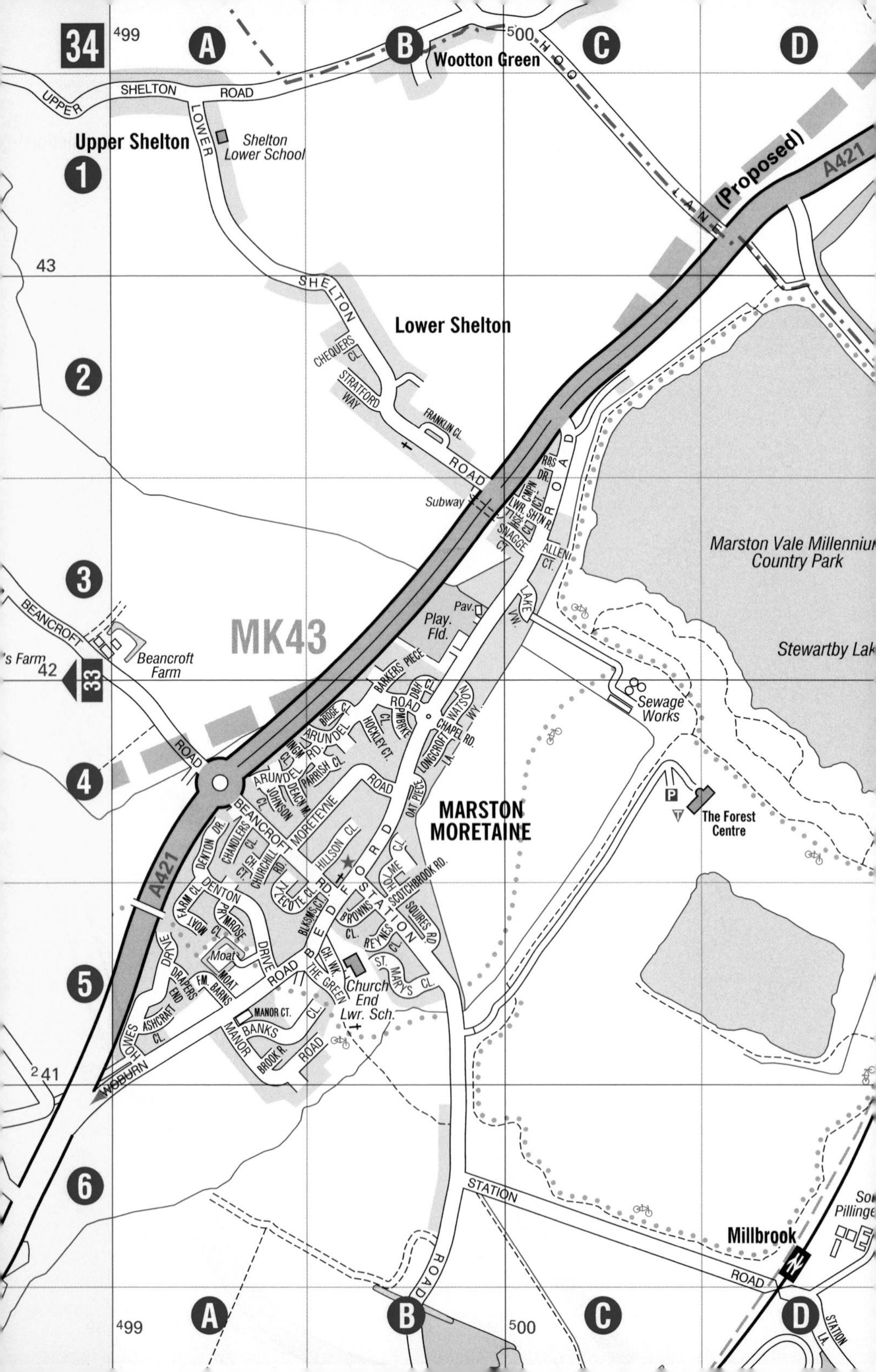

499
A
B
C
D
Wootton Green
500
UPPER SHELTON ROAD
LOWER
Upper Shelton
Shelton Lower School
(Proposed)
A421
43
SHELTON
Lower Shelton
CHEQUERS CL.
STRATFORD WAY
FRANKLIN CL.
ROAD
Subway
RBS DR.
CMPN. CT.
LWR. SHTN. R.
SNAGGE CT.
ALLEN CT.
Marston Vale Millennium Country Park
BEANCROFT ROAD
MK43
Beancroft Farm
's Farm
42
33
Pav.
Play. Fld.
LAKE VW.
Stewartby Lake
BARKERS PIECE
DBH CL.
ROAD PMBRKE
WATSON WY.
Sewage Works
BRDGE CL.
ARUNDEL
HOCKLEY CT.
CHAPEL RD.
LA.
LONGCROFT
PARRISH CL.
ARUNDEL RD.
JOHNSON CL.
MORETEYNE ROAD
OAT PIECE
MARSTON MORETAINE
The Forest Centre
BEANCROFT
DENTON DR.
CHANDLERS CL.
CH. CT.
CHURCHILL RD.
HILLSON CL.
HOLME CL.
SCOTCHBROOK RD.
A421
MOAT FARM CL.
DENTON
PRIMROSE CL.
BEDFORD RD.
STATION
BROWNS CL.
REYNES CL.
SQUIRES RD.
Moat
MOAT
DRIVE
ROAD
CH. WK.
THE GREEN
ST. MARY'S CL.
DRAPERS END
FM. BARNS
Church End Lwr. Sch.
MANOR CT.
ASHCRAFT CL.
HOWES
BANKS CL.
MANOR
BROOK R.
ROAD
WOBURN
41
6
STATION ROAD
Millbrook
Sou Pillinge
ROAD
A
B
C
D
499
500
STATION LA.
1
2
3
4
5
6

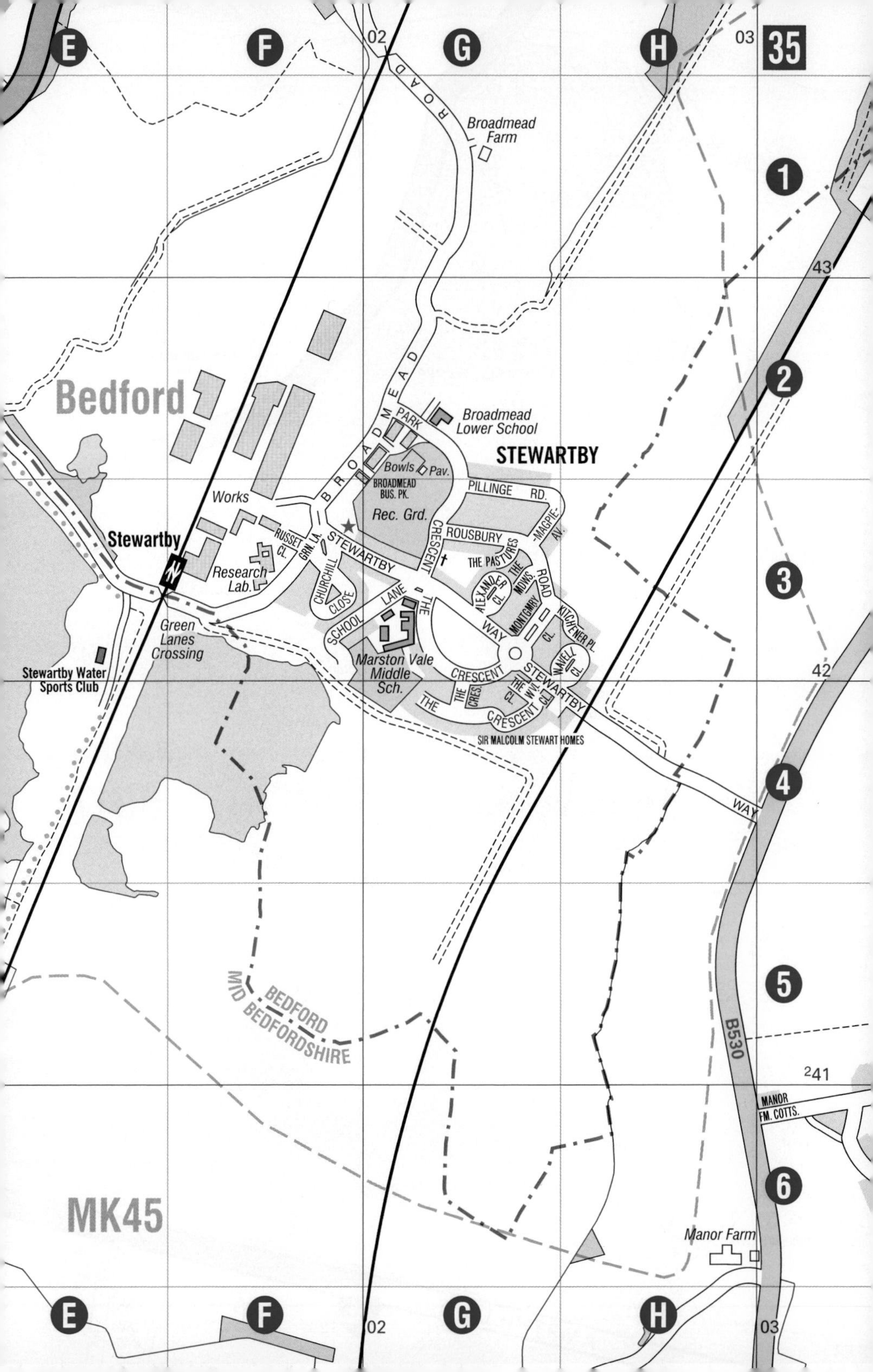

**1**

43'

Broadmead
Farm

**2**

**Bedford**

Broadmead
Lower School

**STEWARTBY**

**Works**

BROADMEAD
BUS. PK.

Bowls Pav.

BROADMEAD PARK

Rec. Grd.

PILLINGE RD.

**Stewartby**

ROUSBURY

MAGPIE AV.

THE PASTURES

**3**

Research
Lab.

RUSSET CL.
GRN LA.

STEWARTBY

CRESCENT

ROAD

ALEXANDER CL.

THE MUNS

KICHNER PL.

Green
Lanes
Crossing

CHURCHILL CLOSE

SCHOOL LANE

THE

WAY

MONTGOMY

WAVELY CL.

42

Stewartby Water
Sports Club

Marston Vale
Middle
Sch.

THE CRESCENT

STEWARTBY

THE WAY CL.

**4**

THE CRESCENT

SIR MALCOLM STEWART HOMES

WAY

BEDFORD
M/D BEDFORDSHIRE

**5**

B530

241

MANOR
FM. COTTS.

**6**

**MK45**

Manor Farm

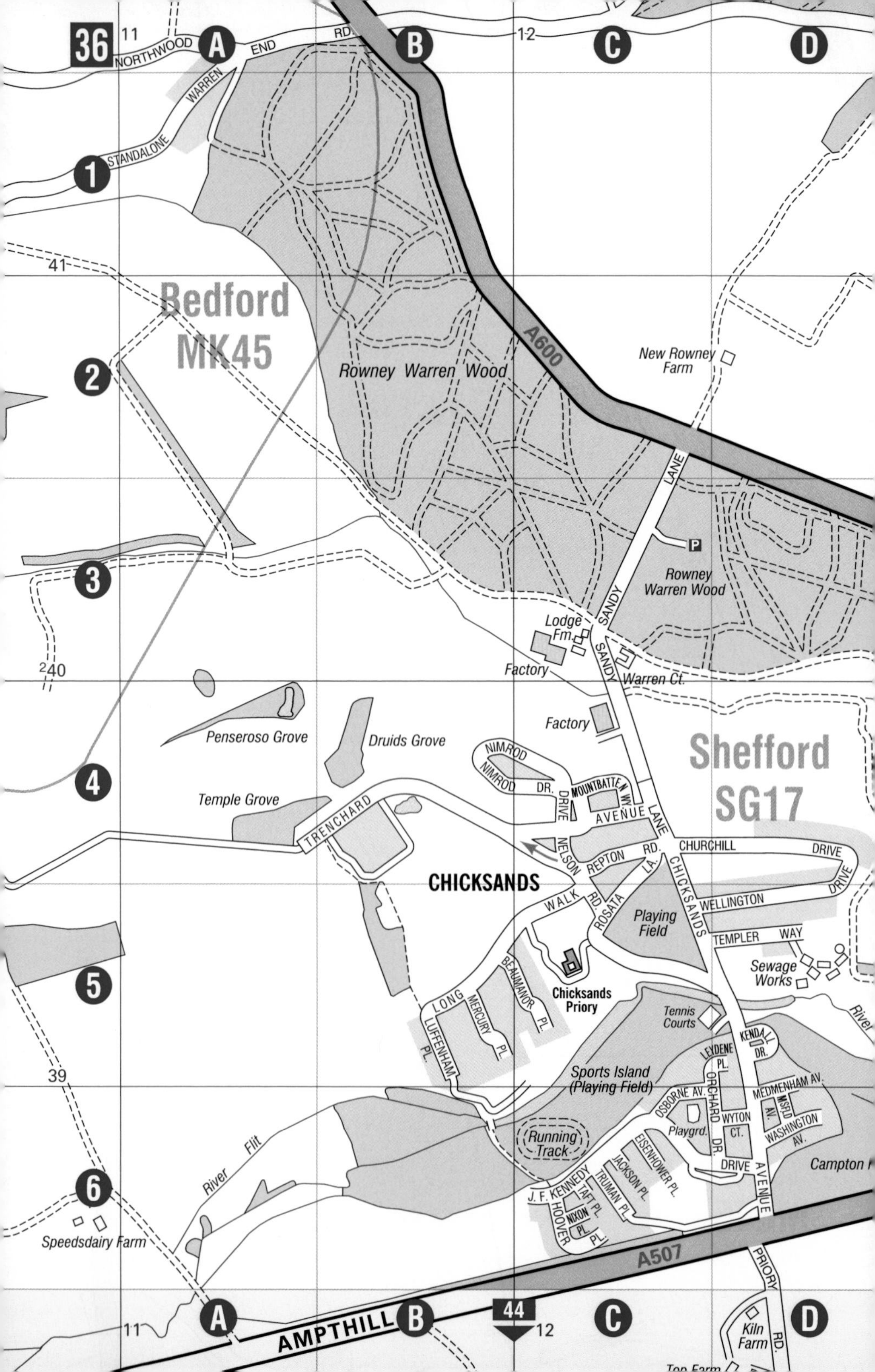

11
NORTHWOOD
END
RD.
12
A
B
C
D
WARREN
STANDALONE
1
2
3
4
5
6
41
40
39
Bedford
MK45
Rowney Warren Wood
A600
New Rowney
Farm
LANE
P
Rowney
Warren Wood
SANDY
Lodge
Fm.
Factory
SANDY
Warren Ct.
Factory
Shefford
SG17
Penseroso Grove
Druids Grove
NIMROD
NIMROD
DR.
DRIVE
MOUNTBATTEN WY.
AVENUE
LANE
Temple Grove
TRENCHARD
NELSON
REPTON
RD.
CHURCHILL
DRIVE
CHICKSANDS
LA.
CHICKSANDS
DRIVE
WALK
RD.
ROSATA
Playing
Field
WELLINGTON
TEMPLER
WAY
Sewage
Works
BEAUMANOR
PL.
Chicksands
Priory
LONG
MERCURY
PL.
LUFFENHAM
PL.
Tennis
Courts
River
KENDALL
DR.
LEYDENE
PL.
Sports Island
(Playing Field)
ORCHARD
DR.
MEDMENHAM AV.
MSFD
AV.
OSBORNE AV.
WYTON
CT.
WASHINGTON
AV.
Playgrd.
Running
Track
River
Flit
EISENHOWER PL.
JACKSON PL.
TRUMAN PL.
DRIVE
AVENUE
Campton
J. F. KENNEDY
TAFT PL.
HOOVER
NIXON
PL.
PL.
Speedsdairy Farm
A507
PRIORY
AMPTHILL
44
11
12
Kiln
Farm
RD.
Top Farm

## Map labels

**Biggleswade SG18**

**SHEFFORD**

### Grid references (top and sides)
E  F  14  G  Southill Park  H  515  **37**

41

② 
③ 
**38** ²40
④ 
⑤ 39
⑥ 
① 
②

E  F  **45**  14  G  H  515

### Features and place names
Ireland Spinney
Moorhall Covert
Stanfordbury Farm
Cockshoothill Grove
Collin's Grove
Bury Spinney
Windmill (disused)
Bellco Meadows

### Roads
BEDFORD B658
A600
A507
GREENWAY
STANFORD ROAD
ROAD
HITCHIN ROAD

### Shefford area streets
GREAT THILL
JUBILEE PL
MOUNT WY
GREAT HAM WY
LUCAS
LUCAS WY
CORNISH CL
HARDWICK CL
RIVERSIDE
POWELLS RD
North Bridge
Shefford Hardwicke
North Bridge
THE WHARF
NORTH BRIDGE ST
BYRNES M.
SHEFFORD BUS. PK.
KINGSMEDE
SHEFFORD BUS. STATION
AYE M.
MAX FIELDS
BARBER END
BLISS
SULLIVAN CL
GREG AV
WEBBER CL
BRITTEN RD
TIPPET CL
ELGAR
WALTON CL
BURY
PURCELL CL
DRIVE
TOWN MDW. CL
PALMER CL
THE HOLLIES
Warehouse
ST.
SOUTHBRIDGE
CLIFTON
ST. FRANCIS WK
Super-ivel store
COOPERS CT.
OAK WOOD RD
QUEENS CT.
DIGSWELL CL
VICTORIA CL
CEDAR CL
NENE MEAD CL
SOUTHFIELDS
PEARTREE CL
HOME MEAD
MAPLE DR
SOUARES CL
Lodge School
PRIORY GATE
AMPTHILL
PENFOLD CL
Cemy.
CAMPTON RD.
Subway
HAZEL CL
SCHOOL LN
BENTLEY M.
WYNCHWOOD CL.
BLOOMFIELD DR.
BRAMLEY CL.
OSBORN CR.
GEORGE ST.
NEW ST.
MID LAND GNS.
Shefford Lwr. Sch.
Robert Bloomfield Mid. Sch.
KING FISHER
MALLARD
NIGHTINGALE M.
HERON CL
SWALLOW CL
ARNHEIM
ALAMEIN
BRIDGE WAY
CHURCHILL
Shefford Ind. Park
BOWL. GRN.
ELM RD
WILLOW WY.
BEECHWOOD RISE
QUEEN ELZBTH CL
SPYTHE RD.
Hall Play. Fld.
Playing Field
SHEFFORD RD.
IVEL RD

**38**

515
16

**A**  **B**  **C**  **D**

**1**

41

STANFORD ROAD

Stanford Farm

BROOM ROAD
B658

THE CRESCENT
OLD SCHOOL LA.
GALPIN CT.
MILL

**Stanford**

RO

**2**

Stanfordbury Farm

Village Farm

**3**

Road

240
**37**
ury Spinney

**4**
STANFORD RD.
B658

STANFORD

Road

Cricket Grd.
Pav.

Clifton Bury Farm
ST.
CLIFTON
FM. BARNS
Clifton Fa
SEARS

Windmill (disused)

River Ivel Navigation (disused)

Clifton Manor

Cemetery

**Shefford SG17**

LYCHMEAD
CHURCH
BATH
CL.
BILBERRY TER.
RECTORY
STOCKBRIDGE
LANE
STREET
WHISTON

**CLIFTON**

**5**
Bellcote Mdws.

BARBER END
BLISS
GREGG AV.
SULLIVAN CL.
ELGAR
39
BRITTEN RD.
TIPPETT CL.
WALTON CL.
PURCELL DRIVE
BURY RD.
NIMROCK's WAY
DR.
**SHEFFORD**
SEFTON FIELDS
SPRING RD.
MANOR CL.
BURROWS
GRANGE LANE
LIME TREE RD.
Pavilion
Play. Fld.
CLIFTON HOUSE
Sch.
MILES
ROOKERY WK.
YEW
OLIVER DB.
WHK.

**6**
CLIFTON RD.
DIGSWELL CL.
ORA RD.
Bowl. Grn.
Play. Fld.
RD.
HITCHIN
CEDAR CL.
OAK END
PEARTREE CL.
HOMEMEAD NE
SOUTHFIELDS CT.
SOUTHFIELDS
MAPLE DR.
SQUIRES CL.
HIDE RD.
SHEFFORD ROAD
PEDLEY
Sports Hall
Games Ct.
Samuel Whitbread Community College
CHAPEL CL.
MAPLE CL.
KNOLLS WAY
BIRCH CL.
BUNYAN CL.
ALEXANDER CL.
FAIRFAX CL.
HARBROOK LANE
CHURCH ST.
OLD SCH. CL.
UBB. CL.
LEE CL.
FAIRGROUND WY.
BROAD
ROAD
NEW ST.
CRES.
THE JOINT
HITCHIN LA.

ROAD

515
**A**

**B**
**46**
16

**C**

NEW

**D**

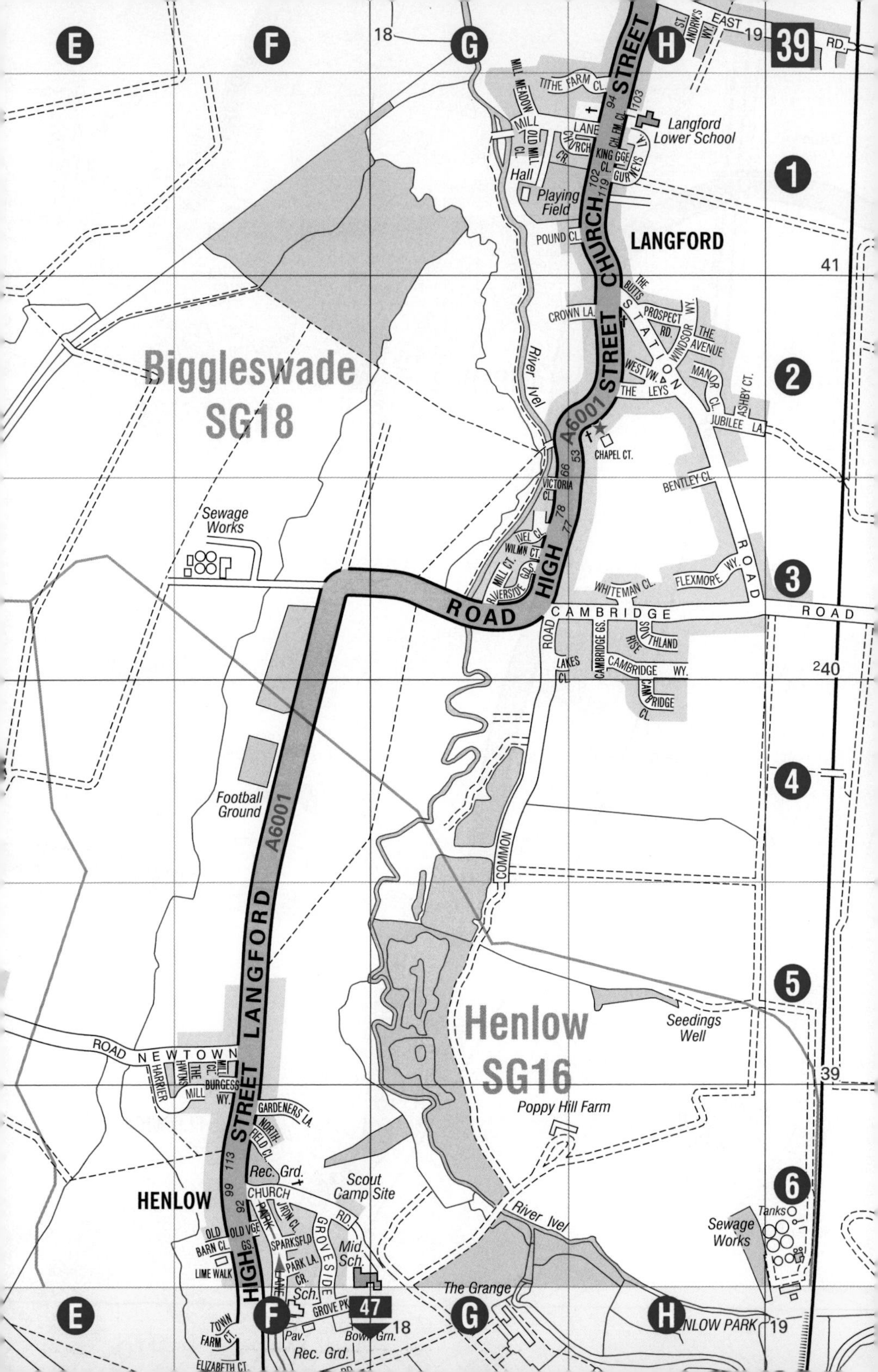

39
Biggleswade
SG18
Henlow
SG16
LANGFORD
HENLOW
CHURCH STREET
HIGH STREET
HIGH ROAD
LANGFORD ROAD
A6001
CAMBRIDGE ROAD
STATION ROAD
Langford Lower School
Playing Field
Hall
TITHE FARM CL.
MILL MEADOW
MILL LANE
OLD MILL CL.
CHURCH CR.
KING GGE CL.
GURNEYS
POUND CL.
ST. ANDREW'S WY.
EAST RD.
CROWN LA.
THE BUTTS
PROSPECT RD.
WINDSOR WY.
THE AVENUE
WEST VW.
THE LEYS
MANOR CL.
ASHBY CT.
JUBILEE LA.
CHAPEL CT.
VICTORIA CL.
BENTLEY CL.
IVEL CL.
WILMN CT.
MILL CT.
RIVERSIDE GDS.
WHITEMAN CL.
FLEXMORE WY.
CAMBRIDGE GS.
SOUTHLAND RISE
LAKES CL.
CAMBRIDGE WY.
CAMBRIDGE CL.
River Ivel
Sewage Works
Football Ground
COMMON
Seedings Well
Poppy Hill Farm
NEWTOWN ROAD
HARRIER
MILL CL.
BURGESS WY.
GARDENERS LA.
NORTHFIELD CL.
Rec. Grd.
Scout Camp Site
CHURCH RD.
PARK LANE
GROVESIDE
SPARKSFLD.
PARK LA. CR.
Mid. Sch.
Sch.
GROVE PK
OLD BARN CL.
OLD VGE GS.
LIME WALK
TOWN FARM CT.
ELIZABETH CT.
Pav.
Bowl Grn.
The Grange
HENLOW PARK
Tanks
47

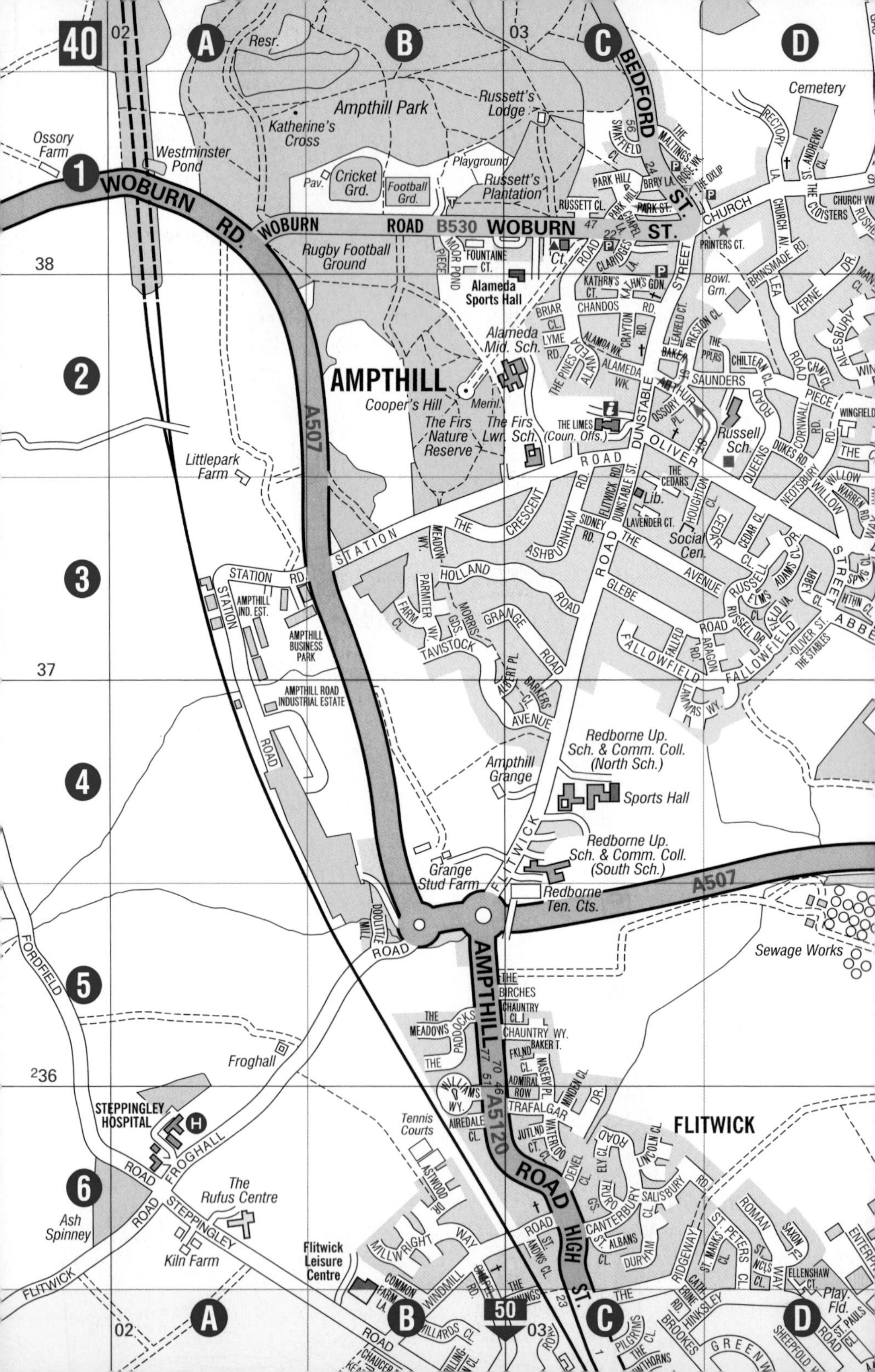

A
B
C
D
02
03
Resr.
Ampthill Park
Katherine's Cross
Russett's Lodge
Cemetery
Ossory Farm
Westminster Pond
Playground
Cricket Grd.
Football Grd.
Pav.
Russett's Plantation
WOBURN RD.
WOBURN ROAD
B530
WOBURN ST.
BEDFORD ST.
Rugby Football Ground
Alameda Sports Hall
Alameda Mid. Sch.
AMPTHILL
Cooper's Hill
Meml.
The Firs Nature Reserve
The Firs Lwr. Sch.
THE LIMES (Coun. Offs.)
Russell Sch.
Lib.
Social Cen.
Bowl. Grn.
PRINTERS CT.
CHURCH ST.
DUNSTABLE ST.
A507
Littlepark Farm
STATION RD.
STATION ROAD
AMPTHILL IND. EST.
AMPTHILL BUSINESS PARK
AMPTHILL ROAD INDUSTRIAL ESTATE
38
37
2 36
Redborne Up. Sch. & Comm. Coll. (North Sch.)
Sports Hall
Ampthill Grange
Redborne Up. Sch. & Comm. Coll. (South Sch.)
Grange Stud Farm
Redborne Ten. Cts.
Sewage Works
AMPTHILL ROAD
A5120
FLITWICK
HIGH ST.
Froghall
STEPPINGLEY HOSPITAL
The Rufus Centre
Ash Spinney
Kiln Farm
Flitwick Leisure Centre
Tennis Courts
FORDFIELD ROAD
FROGHALL ROAD
STEPPINGLEY ROAD
FLITWICK ROAD
Play. Fld.
50

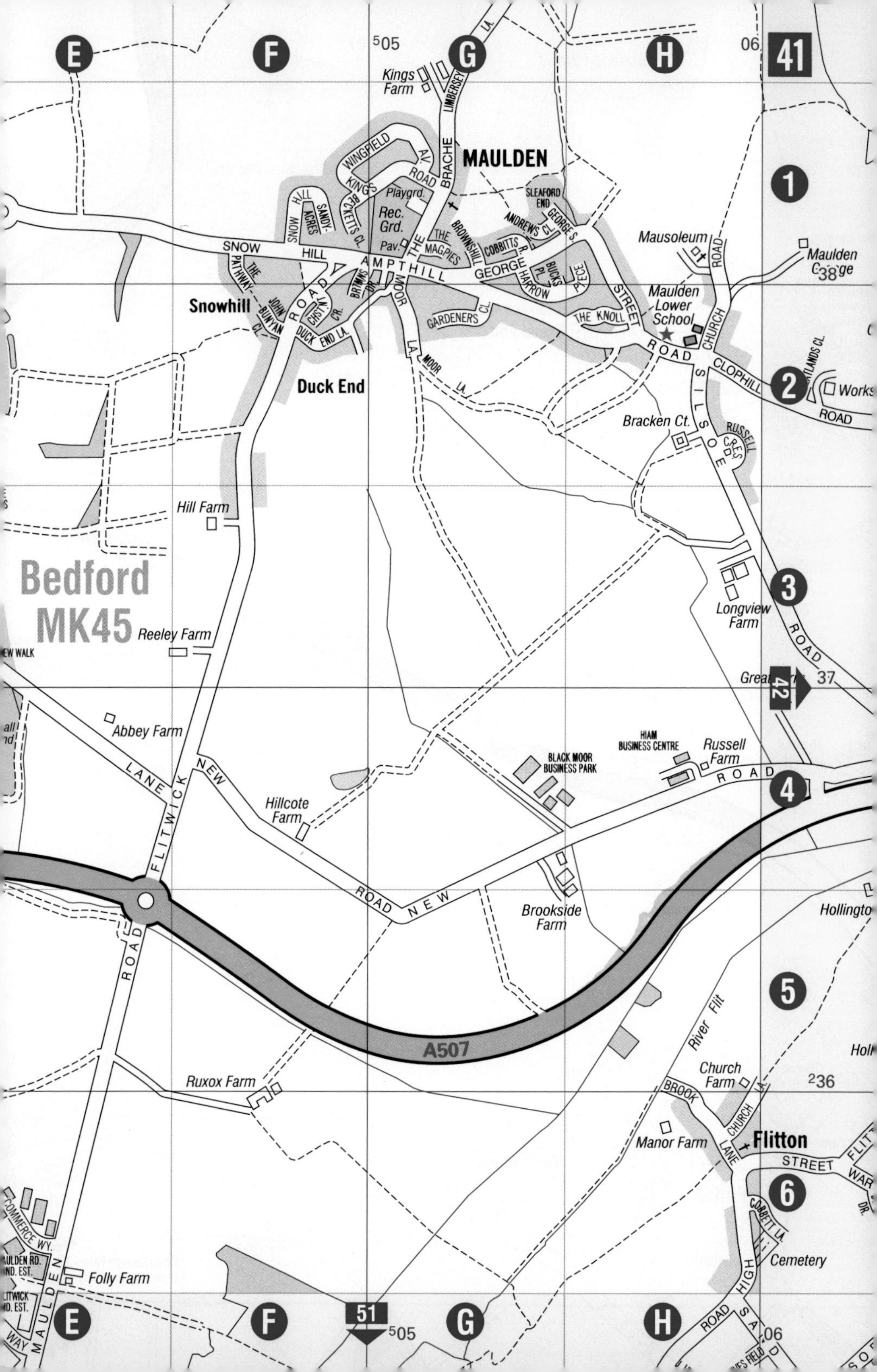
E
F
505
G
H
06
Kings Farm
LIMBERSEY LA.
MAULDEN
WINGFIELD AV.
ROAD
BRACHE
KINGS
BECKETTS CL.
Playgrd.
Rec. Grd.
Pav.
SNOW HILL
SANDY ACRES
SNOW HILL
AMPTHILL
THE MAGPIES
BROWNSHILL
COBBITTS R.
GEORGE
ANDREWS CL.
SLEAFORD END
GEORGES.
HARROW
BUCKS PL.
PIECE
THE PATHWAY
JOHN BUNYAN CL.
ROAD
CHSTNT. CR.
BRIMS DR.
MOOR LA.
THE MOOR
GARDENERS CL.
THE KNOLL
STREET
Mausoleum
ROAD
Maulden Cottage
38
Maulden Lower School
CHURCH
Snowhill
DUCK END LA.
ROAD
CLOPHILL
ROAD
Works
Duck End
Bracken Ct.
SILSOE
RUSSELL CRES.
Hill Farm
Bedford MK45
Longview Farm
ROAD
Reeley Farm
NEW WALK
Great Park
42
37
Abbey Farm
HIAM BUSINESS CENTRE
BLACK MOOR BUSINESS PARK
Russell Farm
ROAD
LANE
FLITWICK
NEW
Hillcote Farm
ROAD NEW
Brookside Farm
Hollington
ROAD
River Flit
A507
Church Farm
36
Ruxox Farm
BROOK
CHURCH LA.
Manor Farm
LANE
Flitton
STREET
COMMERCE WY.
MAULDEN RD. IND. EST.
FLITWICK IND. EST.
CORBETT LA.
Cemetery
Folly Farm
HIGH
WAY
MAULDEN
ROAD
51
505
1
2
3
4
5
6

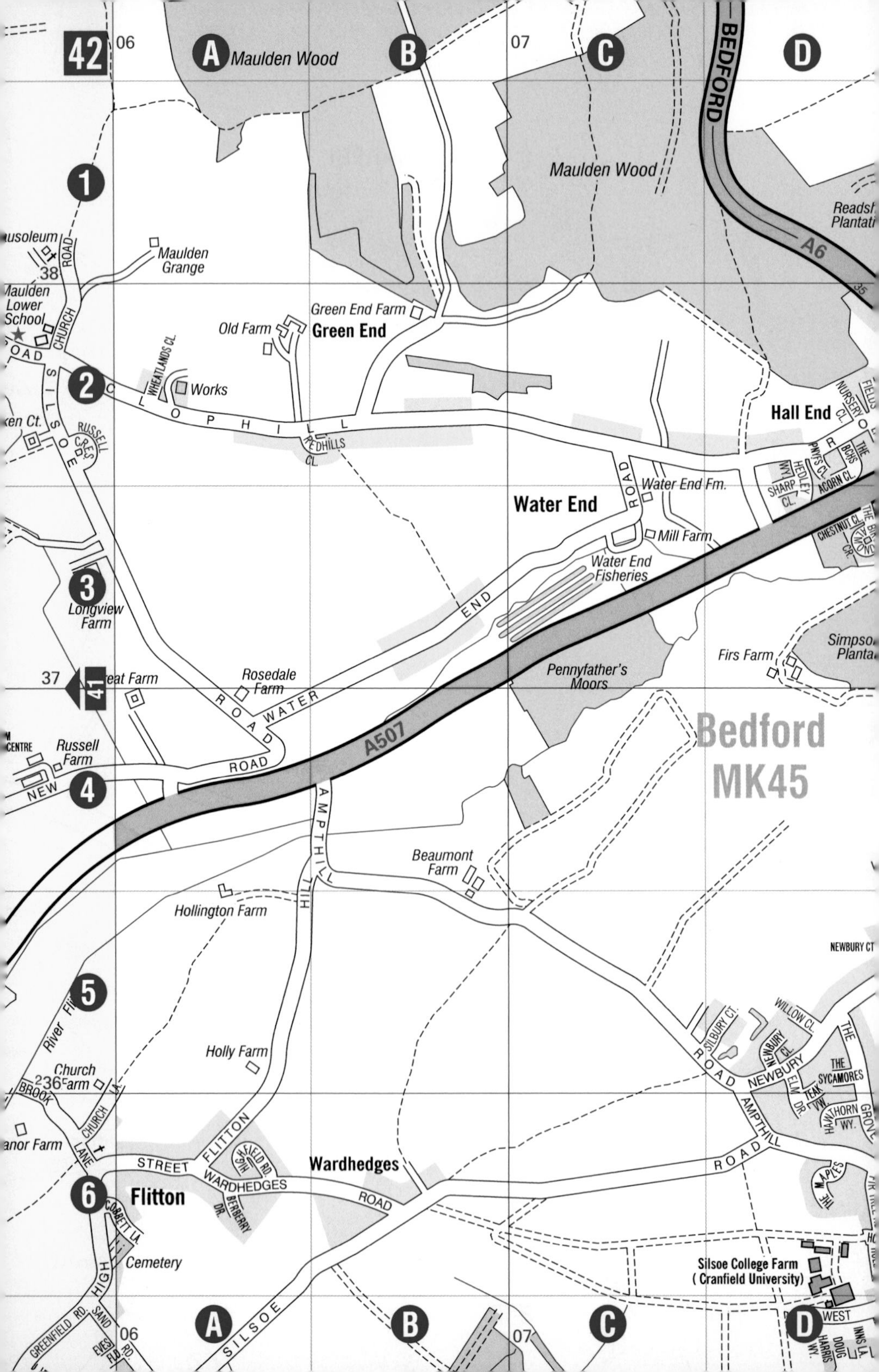

Maulden Wood
Maulden Wood
BEDFORD
A6
Readsfield Plantation
Mausoleum
Maulden Grange
Maulden Lower School
CHURCH ROAD
Green End Farm
Old Farm
Green End
WHEATLANDS CL.
Works
CLOPHILL ROAD
REDHILLS CL.
Hall End
NURSERY CL.
ACORN CL.
SHARP CL.
HEDLEY WY.
CHESTNUT CL.
Water End Fm.
Water End
Mill Farm
Water End Fisheries
RUSSELL CRES.
SILSOE ROAD
Longview Farm
WATER END ROAD
Rosedale Farm
Pennyfather's Moors
Firs Farm
Simpson Plantation
41
Russell Farm
NEW ROAD
A507
Bedford MK45
AMPTHILL ROAD
Beaumont Farm
Hollington Farm
NEWBURY CT.
River Flit
Holly Farm
Church Farm
SILBURY CT.
WILLOW CL.
NEWBURY CL.
NEWBURY ROAD
THE SYCAMORES
ELM DR.
TEAK VW.
HAWTHORN WY.
BROOK LANE
CHURCH LA.
FLITTON
HIGHFIELD RD.
STREET
Wardhedges
WARDHEDGES ROAD
BERBERRY DR.
AMPTHILL ROAD
THE MAPLES
Flitton
CORBETT LA.
Cemetery
Manor Farm
HIGH STREET
Silsoe College Farm
( Cranfield University)
SILSOE ROAD
GREENFIELD RD.
SAND RD.
EVES FLD.
WEST
HARRIS WY.
DOUG
INNS LA.

E
F
G
H
09
510
1
2
3
4
5
6
38
37
236
CLOPHILL
SILSOE
Pine Hill
Playing Field
St. Mary's Lower School
River Flit
Paradise Farm
Sewage Works
Castle Hill
A507
Warren Barns
Warren Wood
Home Farm
Acre Pond
A6
BEDFORD ROAD
ROAD
Pavilion
Silsoe Research Centre
Playing Field
Silsoe Research Centre
Wrest House
Wrest Park Gdns.
Orangery
Cranfield University (Silsoe Campus)
OLD KILN LA.
THE SLADE
LITTLE LANE
GREAT LANE
OLD CHURCH PATH
TOWN M.
TOWNSHOTT
CHURCH MEWS
STREET
SHEFFORD ROAD
JACQUES LANE
CASTLE HILL CT.
HAWTHORNE CL.
MILL LANE
KILN
STREET
CAINHOE
GOODHALL CR.
TANQUERAY AV.
ROAD
READSHILL
BEVERLEY CT.
HIGH
THE CAUSEWAY
OLD SILSOE RD.
GOODWOOD CL.
WARREN LANE
HIGH STREET
JUNIPER CL.
BEDFORD AV.
SCH. HO. MEWS
THE ROWANS
WREST PARK
WREST PK.
CHURCH RD.
ROAD
POPLAR CL.
THE BEECHES

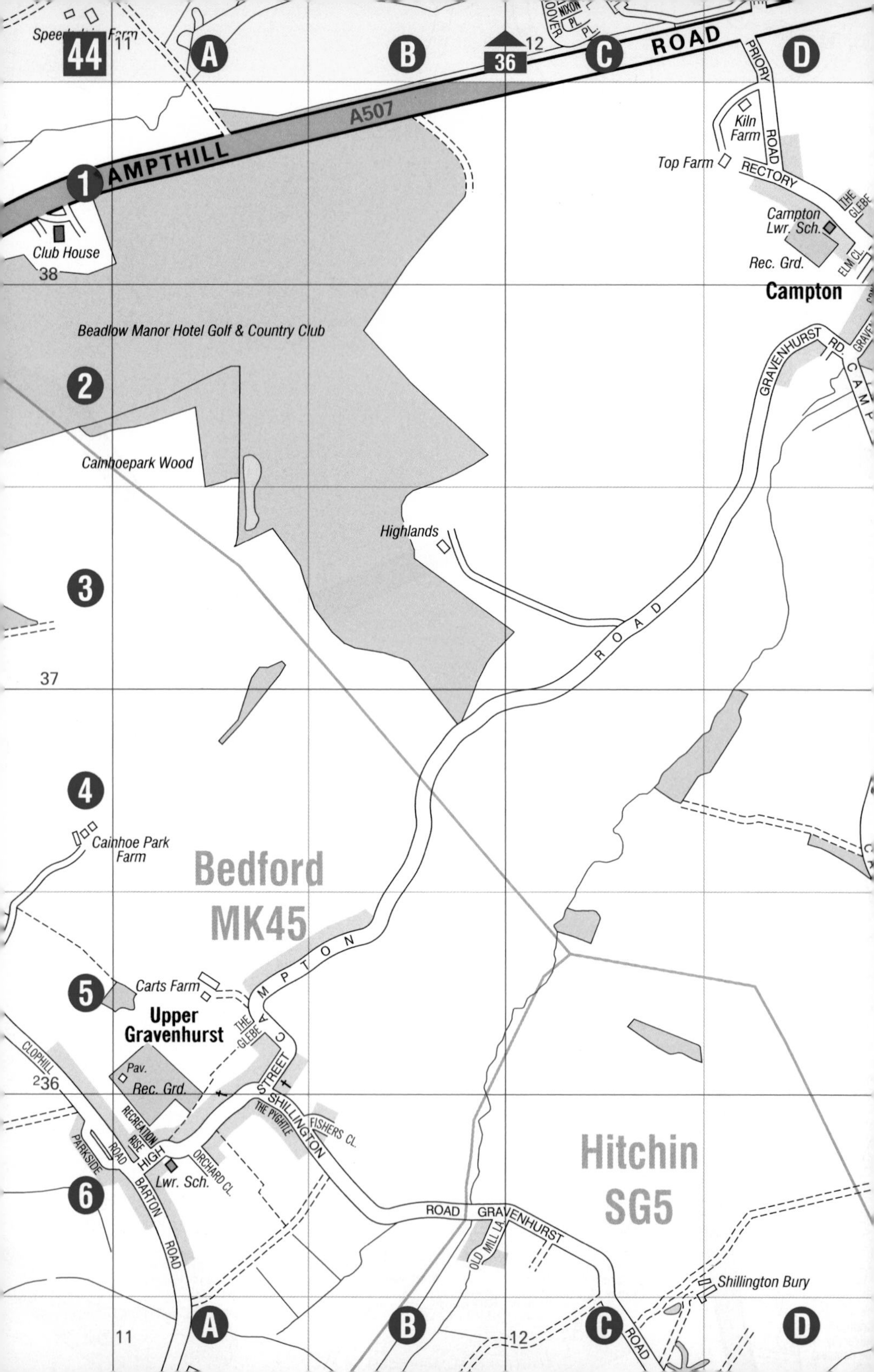

A
B
C
D
36
12
11
ROAD
PRIORY
AMPTHILL
A507
Kiln Farm
ROAD
Top Farm
RECTORY
THE GLEBE
Campton Lwr. Sch.
Rec. Grd.
ELM CL.
Campton
Club House
38
Beadlow Manor Hotel Golf & Country Club
GRAVENHURST RD.
CAMP
Cainhoepark Wood
Highlands
ROAD
37
Cainhoe Park Farm
Bedford MK45
CAMPTON
Carts Farm
Upper Gravenhurst
THE GLEBE
STREET
CLOPHILL
36
Pav.
Rec. Grd.
RECREATION RISE
HIGH
SHILLINGTON
THE PYGHTLE
FISHERS CL.
Hitchin SG5
PARKSIDE
ROAD
BARTON
ROAD
Lwr. Sch.
ORCHARD CL.
ROAD
GRAVENHURST
OLD MILL LA.
Shillington Bury
ROAD
11
12
1
2
3
4
5
6

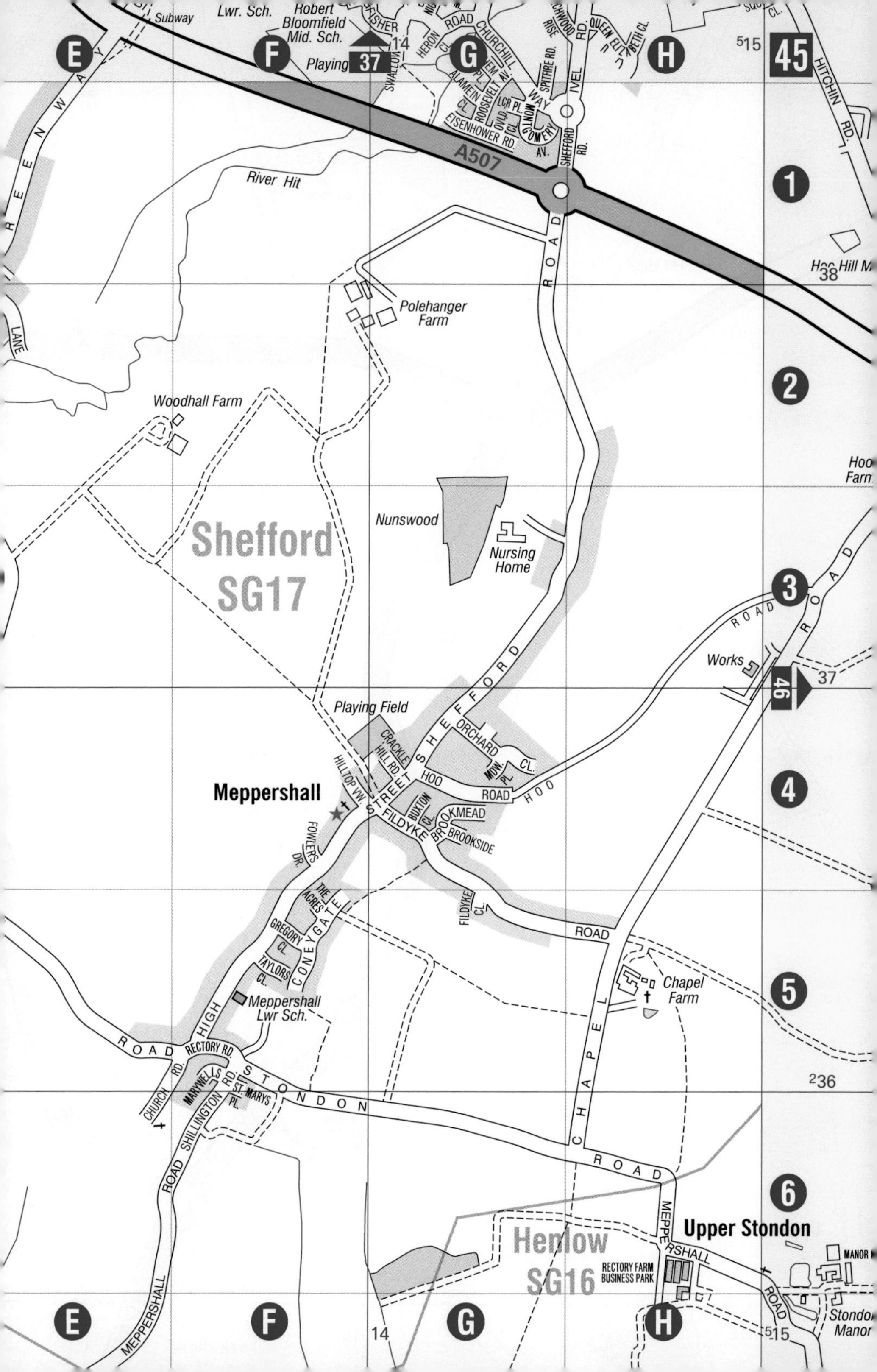

Subway
Lwr. Sch.
Robert
Bloomfield
Mid. Sch.
Playing
37

**E** **F** **G** **H**

**45**

CHURCHILL
SWALLOW
HERON
ROAD
KINGFISHER
SPITFIRE RD.
IVEL
QUEEN CL.
BETTI CL.

515

HITCHIN RD.

A507

**1**

River Hit

Hoo Hill M
38

Polehanger
Farm

**2**

Woodhall Farm

Hoo
Farm

**Shefford
SG17**

Nunswood

Nursing
Home

ROAD

ROAD

**3**

Works
46
37

Playing Field

SHEFFORD

ORCHARD
CL.

HOO

**4**

**Meppershall**

HILLTOP VW.
CRACKLE HILL RD.
STREET
HOO
BUXTON
MOW PL.
ROAD
BROOKMEAD
BROOKSIDE

FOWLERS DR.
FILDYKE
FILDYKE CL.

ROAD

Chapel
Farm

**5**

THE ACRES
CONEYGATE
GREGORY CL.
TAYLORS CL.

236

ROAD

HIGH

Meppershall
Lwr. Sch.

RECTORY RD.
STONDON

CHURCH RD.
MAXWELLS
SHILLINGTON RD.
ST. MARYS PL.

CHAPEL

ROAD

**6**

MEPPERSHALL

**Upper Stondon**

MANOR

**Henlow
SG16**

RECTORY FARM
BUSINESS PARK

ROAD

515
Stondon
Manor

**E** 14 **F** **G** **H**

MEPPERSHALL

**46** 515

**A** **B** **38** 16 **C** **D**

HITCHIN ROAD

BROAD

HITCHIN LA

CL.

**1**

CLIFTON PARK

NEW ROAD

38

Hoo Hill Maze

Wren Park

A507

**2**

A507

Hoo Farm

Shefford
SG17

ROAD

**3**

ROAD

Works

A600

HOO

Works

37 **45**

HENLOW   AIRFIELD

CHAPEL

**4**

Butts
(Rifle Range)

Stanpit
House

Henlow Golf Course

BEDFORD

**5** Chapel
Farm

CAMP

236

HITCHIN

Nursery

WHITE

TEDDE

Henlow
Greyhound
Stadium

P

OLDFIELD

BURNETT

KAREN
HO.

**6**

Upper Stondon

MANOR FARM

ROAD

HENLOW
IND. EST.

ALTON
RD.

BORTON

MILL
CL.

A600 ROAD

ASTRAL
AV.

MEPPERSHALL

Stondon Mnr.

STATION

Pavilion

WILLOW TREES
CARAVAN SITE

PECKWORTH
IND. EST.

Ple

515

RD.

**A** **B** 16 **C** **D**

BIRCH GRO.

THREE STAR PARK

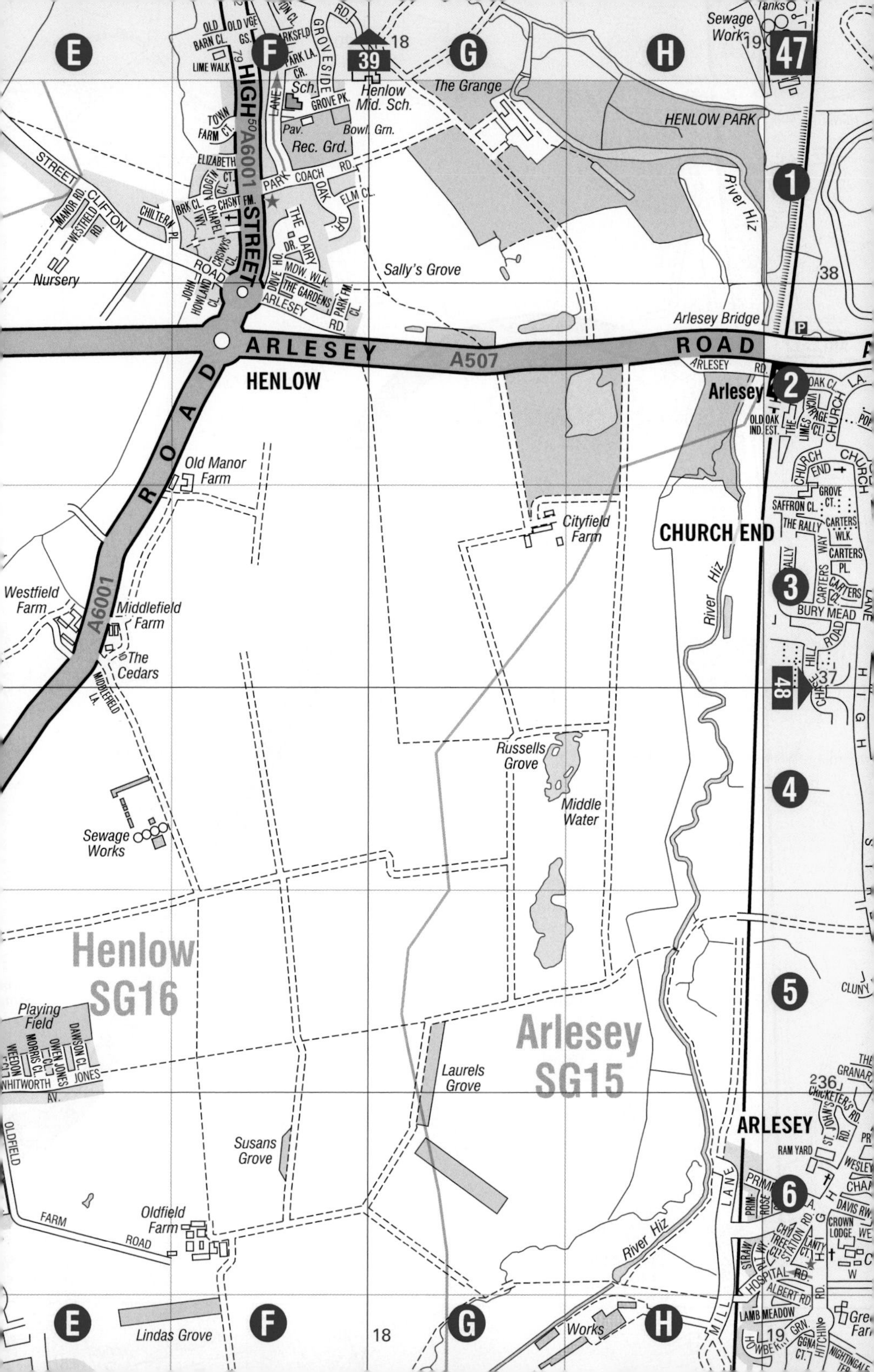

E
F
G
H
47
39
18
HIGH STREET
A6001
HENLOW PARK
The Grange
Henlow Mid. Sch.
Rec. Grd.
Sewage Works
River Hiz
Sally's Grove
Arlesey Bridge
ARLESEY ROAD
A507
HENLOW
Arlesey
CHURCH END
Old Manor Farm
Cityfield Farm
Westfield Farm
Middlefield Farm
The Cedars
Nursery
CLIFTON ROAD
Russells Grove
Middle Water
Henlow SG16
Arlesey SG15
Playing Field
Laurels Grove
Susans Grove
Oldfield Farm
OLDFIELD FARM ROAD
Lindas Grove
Works
ARLESEY
MILL LANE
1
2
3
4
5
6
38
37
48
236

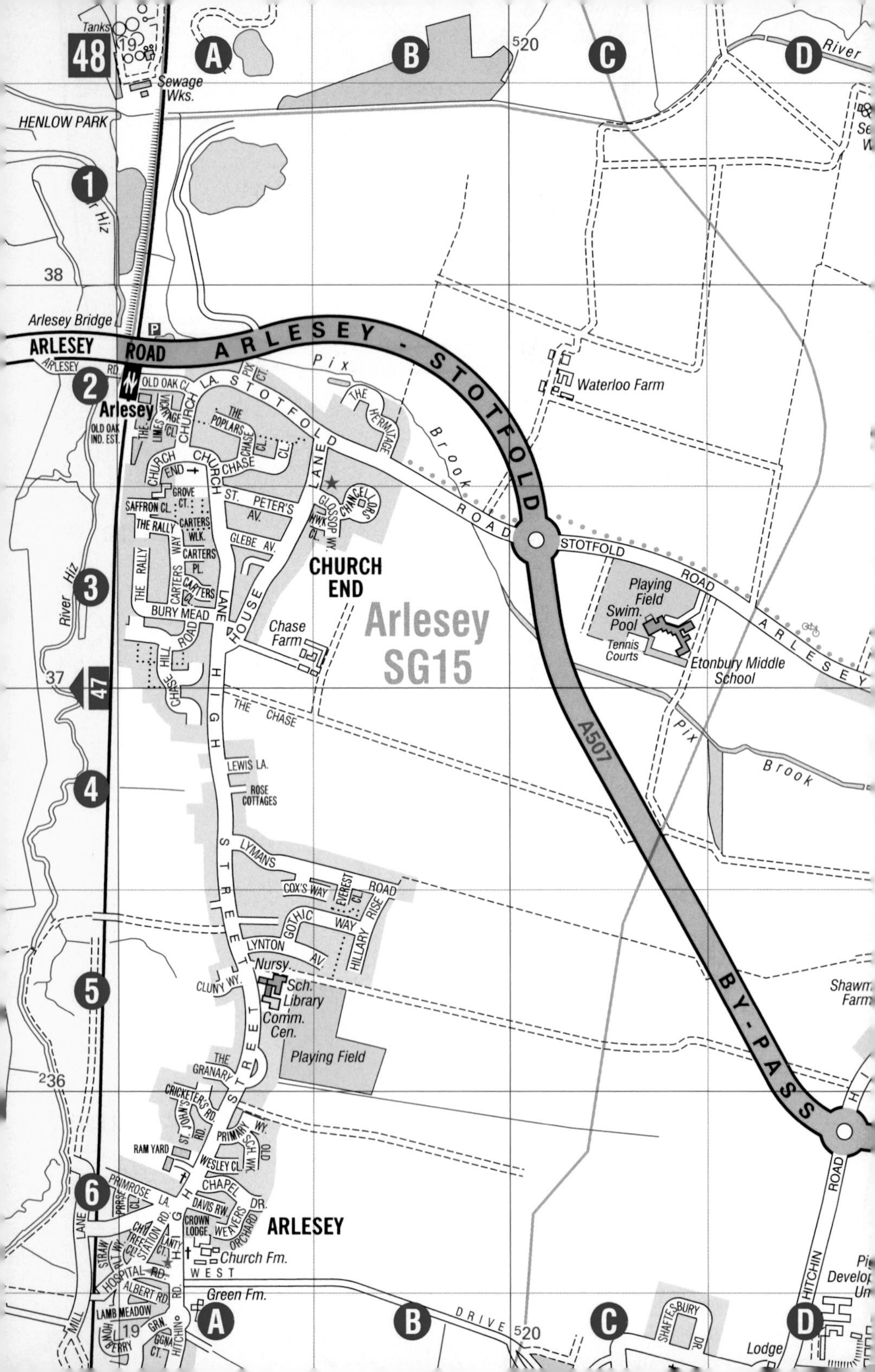
48
Tanks
Sewage Wks.
HENLOW PARK
A
B
C
D
520
River
1
2
3
4
5
6
38
37
36
19
47
River Hiz
Arlesey Bridge
ARLESEY ROAD
ARLESEY - STOTFOLD
ARLESEY RD.
Arlesey
OLD OAK IND. EST.
OLD OAK CL.
CHURCH LA.
STOTFOLD ROAD
PIX CT.
THE HERMITAGE
Pix Brook
Waterloo Farm
THE POPLARS
CHASE CL.
CHURCH CHASE
CHURCH END
CHANCELLORS
GLOSSOP WY.
HWK. CL.
ST. PETER'S AV.
GLEBE AV.
GROVE CT.
SAFFRON CL.
THE RALLY
CARTERS WLK.
CARTERS PL.
CARTERS WAY
CARTERS CL.
BURY MEAD
LANE
HOUSE
HILL
ROAD
CHASE
CHURCH END
Arlesey SG15
Chase Farm
STOTFOLD ROAD
Playing Field
Swim. Pool
Tennis Courts
Etonbury Middle School
ARLESEY
A507
THE CHASE
HIGH STREET
LEWIS LA.
ROSE COTTAGES
LYMANS
COX'S WAY
EVEREST CL.
ROAD
GOTHIC WAY
RISE
HILLARY
LYNTON AV.
Nursy.
CLUNY WY.
Sch.
Library
Comm. Cen.
Playing Field
BY-PASS
Shawm Farm
THE GRANARY
CRICKETER'S RD.
ST. JOHN'S RD.
PRIMARY WY.
SCH. WK.
OLD
RAM YARD
WESLEY CL.
PRIMROSE LA.
PRSE CL.
CHAPEL DR.
DAVIS RW.
CROWN LODGE
WEAVERS
ORCHARD
ARLESEY
LANE
STRAW
CHE TREE CL.
STATION RD.
LANTY CT.
Church Fm.
HOSPITAL RD.
WEST
DRIVE
ALBERT RD.
Green Fm.
LAMB MEADOW
MILL
GRN.
HITCHIN
GGNA CT.
BERRY
SHAFTESBURY DR.
HITCHIN ROAD
Lodge
Pig Develop Un

Astwick
Church Fm.
Ival
Astwick Bury
Moat
Mill
Mill Ho.
Weir
Swallowfield
Old Mill Cottage
Greenfields
Carrickgreen
Ivel Mill
Taylor's Mill
Cat Ditch
New Inn
Spinney Farm
Chilcotes
Brookside
GREAT NORTH ROAD
Stotfold Common
Mill Race
Baldock SG7
Nursery
Skylarks
Works
Stotfold Green
Playing Field
Football Ground
Hitchin SG5
Radwell Grange Spinney
NORTH HERTFORDSHIRE
MID BEDFORDSHIRE
Ford Bridge
STOTFOLD
Cemetery
School
Stotfold Bury
Bury Farm
Mill Stream
Sch.
Lib.
Mill Race
Weir
Works
New Bridge
Junction 10 A1(M)
BY-PASS
A507
Brook End
Rec. Grd.
Boundary Farm
Mill House
Radwell
Garden Cottages
Capra
Baldock SG7
SG6
Poultry Farm
Radwell Lodge
Pix Brook
LESEY - STOTFOLD
E
F
G
H
22
23
38
37
236
1
2
3
4
5
6

50
40
A
B
C
D
1
2
3
4
5
6
02
03
35
34
33
FLITWICK
WESTONING
Flitwick Leisure Centre
Kiln
STEPPINGLEY ROAD
Flitwick Wood
Wood Farm
Old Farm
Priestley Farm
Moors Plantation
Worthy End Farm
Ckt. Grd.
Pav.
Flitwick
Woodland Middle Sch.
Lwr. Sch.
Lib.
Rec. Grd.
Cemy.
The Mount
Bowling Green
Kingsmoor Prim. Sch.
Play. Fld.
Westoning Manor
Cemetery
Playing Field
Park Fm.
Westoning Lwr. Sch.
A5120
HIGH STREET
DUNSTABLE RD.
FLITWICK ROAD
HIGH ST.
CHURCH ROAD
TEMPLE WAY
PARKWAY DRIVE
MANOR WAY
DEW POND RD.
EASTON RD.
GREENWAYS
SHEEPFOLD HILL
AVENUE
HINKSLEY
STATION SQ.
KING'S
VICARAGE
TOWNFIELD ROAD
HORNES END ROAD
FIR TREE CL.
GREENFIELD ROAD
CHURCH
MANOR PARK DR.
HOME FARM WY.

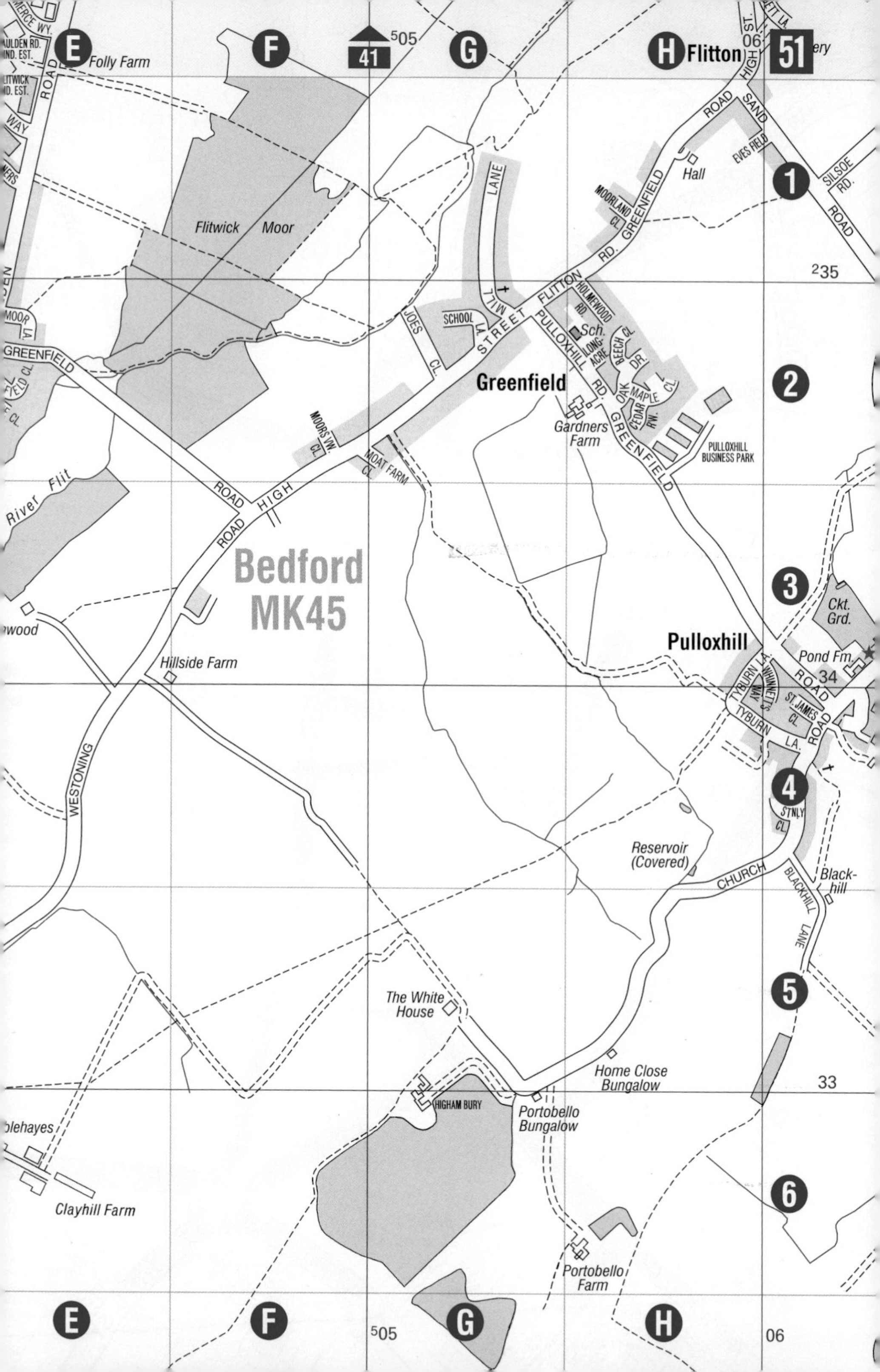

E
F
G
H
41
505
Flitton
51
Folly Farm
Flitwick Moor
Hall
EVES FIELD
SILSOE RD.
ROAD
SAND
HIGH ST.
06
MOORLAND CL.
GREENFIELD RD.
FLITTON
LANE
MILL
STREET
SCHOOL LA.
JOES CL.
HOLMEWOOD RD.
PULLOXHILL RD.
Sch.
LONG ACRE
BEECH CL.
OAK DR.
MAPLE CL.
CEDAR RW.
Greenfield
Gardners Farm
GREENFIELD
PULLOXHILL BUSINESS PARK
MOORS VW. CL.
MOAT FARM CL.
HIGH
ROAD
GREENFIELD
River Flit
Bedford MK45
Hillside Farm
WESTONING
235
1
2
3
Ckt. Grd.
Pulloxhill
Pond Fm.
34
TYBURN LA.
WHINNETT'S WAY
ST. JAMES CL.
TYBURN LA.
ROAD
4
STNLY CL.
Reservoir (Covered)
CHURCH
BLACKHILL
LANE
Black-hill
5
The White House
Home Close Bungalow
33
HIGHAM BURY
Portobello Bungalow
6
Clayhill Farm
Portobello Farm
E
F
505
G
H
06

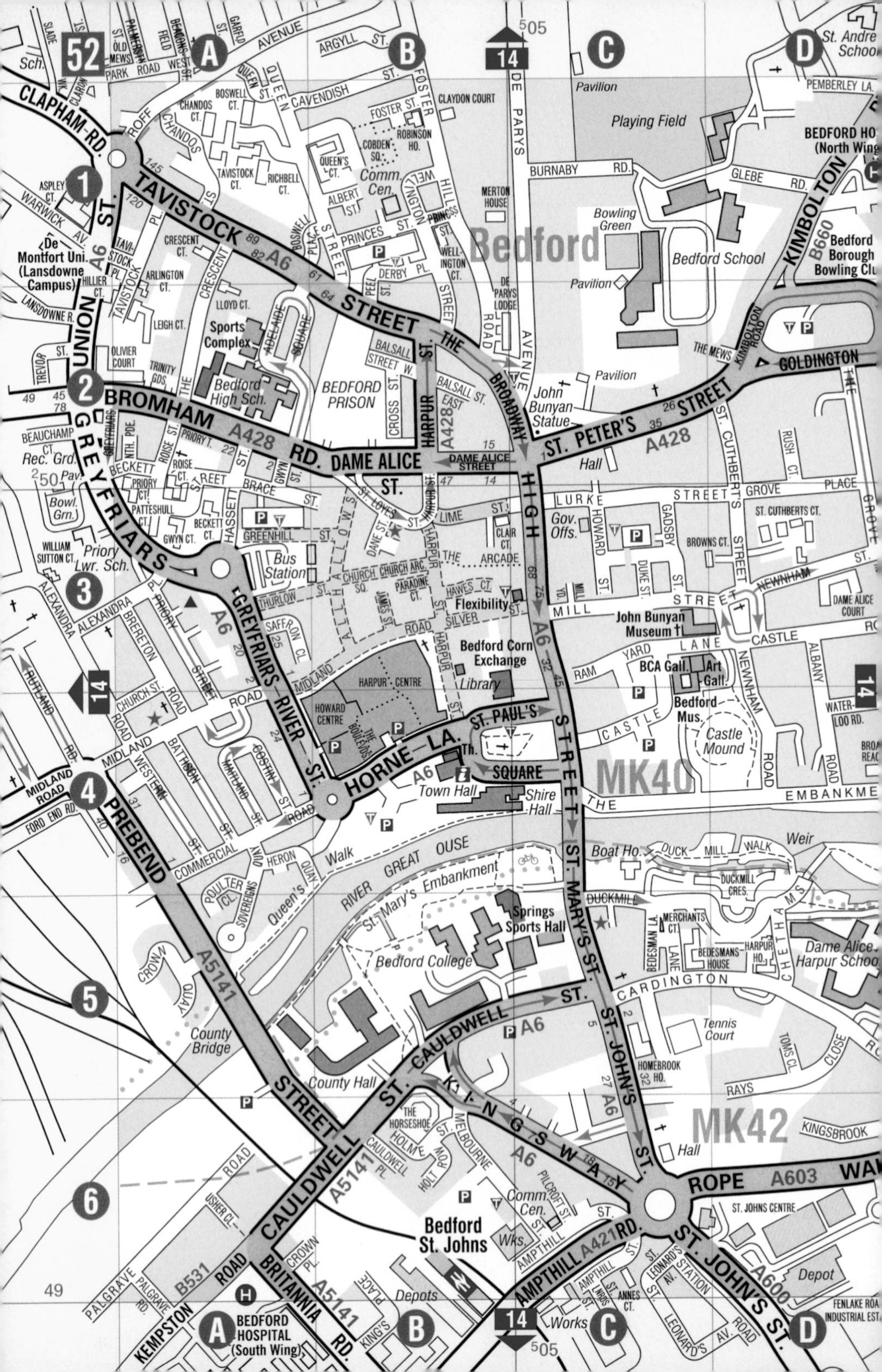

52
A
B
C
D
1
2
3
4
5
6
14
505
Bedford
MK40
MK42
CLAPHAM RD.
TAVISTOCK STREET
A6
UNION ST.
BROMHAM RD.
A428
DAME ALICE ST.
DAME ALICE STREET
GREYFRIARS
HIGH ST.
ST. PETER'S STREET
GOLDINGTON
KIMBOLTON ROAD
B660
THE BROADWAY
DE PARYS AVENUE
BURNABY RD.
GLEBE RD.
PEMBERLEY LA.
ARGYLL ST.
AVENUE
CAVENDISH ST.
FOSTER HILL ROAD
WELLINGTON STREET
PRINCES ST.
DERBY PL.
PEEL ST.
HARPUR ST.
BALSALL STREET W.
BALSALL ST. EAST
CROSS ST.
ADELAIDE SQUARE
CRESCENT
PRIORY ST.
BECKETT ST.
BRACE ST.
HASSETT ST.
GREENHILL ST.
THURLOW ST.
ALLHALLOWS
CHURCH SQ.
CHURCH ARC.
PARADINE CT.
JAMES ST.
SILVER ST.
HAWES CT.
THE ARCADE
LIME ST.
ST. LOYES
LURKE STREET
HOWARD ST.
GADSBY ST.
DUKE ST.
MILL STREET
ST. CUTHBERT'S STREET
GROVE PLACE
RUSH CT.
NEWNHAM ST.
NEWNHAM ROAD
CASTLE LANE
CASTLE RD.
RAM YARD
ALBANY ROAD
WATERLOO RD.
THE EMBANKMENT
ST. PAUL'S SQUARE
HORNE LA.
MIDLAND RD.
RIVER ST.
GREYFRIARS RIVER ST.
PRIORY STREET
ALEXANDRA RD.
RUTLAND RD.
BRERETON ROAD
CHURCH ST.
WESTERN ST.
BATTISON ST.
COSTIN ST.
MAITLAND ST.
COMMERCIAL RD.
QUAY
HERON QUAY
POULTER CL.
SOVEREIGNS
FORD END RD.
PREBEND STREET
A5141
CROWN QUAY
COUNTY Bridge
ST. MARY'S STREET
ST. MARY'S ST.
ST. JOHN'S ST.
DUCK MILL WALK
DUCKMILL LA.
DUCKMILL CRES.
BEDESMAN LA.
CARDINGTON RD.
CAULDWELL ST.
KINGSWAY
THE HORSESHOE
HOLME ST.
HOLT ROW
MELBOURNE ST.
CAULDWELL PL.
PILCROFT ST.
AMPTHILL RD.
A421
ROPE WALK
A603
A600
ST. JOHN'S ST.
ST. LEONARD'S AV.
STATION ROAD
ST. ANNES CT.
KEMPSTON ROAD
B531
BRITANNIA RD.
CROWN PL.
KING'S PLACE
PALGRAVE RD.
USHER CL.
ROAD
TOMS CL.
RAYS CLOSE
KINGSBROOK
HOMEBROOK HO.
Pavilion
Playing Field
Bowling Green
Bedford School
BEDFORD HOSPITAL (North Wing)
St. Andrew's School
Bedford Borough Bowling Club
John Bunyan Statue
Hall
Gov. Offs.
ST. CUTHBERTS CT.
BROWNS CT.
DAME ALICE COURT
John Bunyan Museum
BCA Gall.
Art Gall.
Bedford Mus.
Castle Mound
Bedford Corn Exchange
Library
Flexibility
HARPUR CENTRE
HOWARD CENTRE
THE BOULEVARD
Town Hall
Shire Hall
Bus Station
Sports Complex
Bedford High Sch.
BEDFORD PRISON
Comm. Cen.
QUEEN'S CT.
ALBERT ST.
COBDEN SQ.
ROBINSON HO.
CLAYDON COURT
BOSWELL CT.
CHANDOS CT.
TAVISTOCK CT.
RICHBELL CT.
MERTON HOUSE
DE PARYS LODGE
CRESCENT CT.
ARLINGTON CT.
LLOYD CT.
LEIGH CT.
OLIVIER COURT
TRINITY GDS.
ASPLEY CT.
WARWICK AV.
De Montfort Uni. (Lansdowne Campus)
HILLIER CT.
LANSDOWNE R.
TREVOR ST.
BEAUCHAMP CT.
Rec. Grd.
Pav.
Bowl. Grn.
WILLIAM SUTTON CT.
Priory Lwr. Sch.
PATTESHULL CT.
GWYN CT.
ROISE CT.
NTH. PDE.
SAFFRON CL.
MIDLAND
CLAIR CT.
Boat Ho.
Weir
River Great Ouse
Queen's Walk
St. Mary's Embankment
Springs Sports Hall
Bedford College
MERCHANTS CT.
BEDESMANS HOUSE
HARPUR HO.
CHETHAMS
Dame Alice Harpur School
Tennis Court
County Hall
Bedford St. Johns
Wks.
Depots
Works
ST. JOHNS CENTRE
Depot
FENLAKE ROAD INDUSTRIAL ESTATE
BEDFORD HOSPITAL (South Wing)
THE MEWS
SLADE
PALMERSTON
BEACONS FIELD
PARK ROAD WEST
GARFIELD
QUEEN ST.
ROFF AV.
CLARION
49

# INDEX

Including Streets, Places & Areas, Hospitals & Hospices, Industrial Estates,
Selected Flats & Walkways, Stations and Selected Places of Interest.

## HOW TO USE THIS INDEX

1. Each street name is followed by its Postcode District and then by its Locality abbreviation(s) and then by its map reference;
   e.g. **Abbey Flds.** MK42 Els . . . .2B **26** is in the MK42 Postcode District and the Elstow Locality and is to be found in square 2B on page **26**.
   The page number is shown in bold type.

2. A strict alphabetical order is followed in which Av., Rd., St., etc. (though abbreviated) are read in full and as part of the street name;
   e.g. **Black Hat Cl.** appears after **Blackburn Cl.** but before **Blackhill La.**

3. Streets and a selection of flats and walkways too small to be shown on the maps, appear in the index with the thoroughfare to which it is connected shown in
   brackets; e.g. **Abbots Wlk.** SG18: Big . . . .3F **31** (off High St.)

4. Addresses that are in more than one part are referred to as not continuous.

5. Places and areas are shown in the index in **BLUE TYPE** and the map reference is to the actual map square in which the town centre or area is located and not to the
   place name shown on the map; e.g. **AMPTHILL** . . . .2C **40**

6. An example of a selected place of interest is **John Bunyan Mus.** . . . .3C **52**

7. An example of a station is **Arlesey Station (Rail)** . . . .2A **48**. Included are Rail **(Rail)** and Park & Ride **(Park & Ride)**

8. An example of a hospital or hospice is **BIGGLESWADE HOSPITAL** . . . .1H **31**

9. Map references for entries that appear on large scale page **52** are shown first, with small scale map references shown in brackets;
   e.g. **Adelaide Sq.** MK40: Bed . . . .2A **52** (2B **14**)

## GENERAL ABBREVIATIONS

| | | | |
|---|---|---|---|
| **Arc.** : Arcade | **Est.** : Estate | **Lit.** : Little | **Rd.** : Road |
| **Av.** : Avenue | **Fld.** : Field | **Lwr.** : Lower | **Rdbt.** : Roundabout |
| **Bri.** : Bridge | **Flds.** : Fields | **Mnr.** : Manor | **Sq.** : Square |
| **Bus.** : Business | **Gdn.** : Garden | **Mdw.** : Meadow | **St.** : Street |
| **Cvn.** : Caravan | **Gdns.** : Gardens | **Mdws.** : Meadows | **Ter.** : Terrace |
| **C'way.** : Causeway | **Ga.** : Gate | **M.** : Mews | **Trad.** : Trading |
| **Cen.** : Centre | **Gt.** : Great | **Mt.** : Mount | **Up.** : Upper |
| **Cl.** : Close | **Grn.** : Green | **Mus.** : Museum | **Vw.** : View |
| **Cotts.** : Cottages | **Gro.** : Grove | **Nth.** : North | **Vis.** : Visitors |
| **Ct.** : Court | **Hgts.** : Heights | **Pde.** : Parade | **Wlk.** : Walk |
| **Cres.** : Crescent | **Ho.** : House | **Pk.** : Park | **W.** : West |
| **Cft.** : Croft | **Ind.** : Industrial | **Pas.** : Passage | **Yd.** : Yard |
| **Dr.** : Drive | **Info.** : Information | **Pl.** : Place | |
| **E.** : East | **La.** : Lane | **Ri.** : Rise | |

## LOCALITY ABBREVIATIONS

| | | | |
|---|---|---|---|
| Amp : **Ampthill** | Cran : **Cranfield** | L Sto : **Lower Stondon** | Sil : **Silsoe** |
| Arl : **Arlesey** | Els : **Elstow** | M Mor : **Marston Moretaine** | Sou : **Southill** |
| Ast : **Astwick** | Eve : **Everton** | Mau : **Maulden** | Stan : **Stanford** |
| Bead : **Beadlow** | F'ton : **Flitton** | Mep : **Meppershall** | Step : **Steppingley** |
| Bed : **Bedford** | Flit : **Flitwick** | Mil : **Millbrook** | Stev : **Stevington** |
| Bee : **Beeston** | Gam : **Gamlingay** | Mog : **Moggerhanger** | Stew : **Stewartby** |
| Bid : **Biddenham** | Grav : **Gravenhurst** | Nor : **Norton** | Stot : **Stotfold** |
| Big : **Biggleswade** | G Bar : **Great Barford** | Oak : **Oakley** | Sut : **Sutton** |
| Blun : **Blunham** | Gre : **Greenfield** | O War : **Old Warden** | Tem : **Tempsford** |
| Brom : **Bromham** | Har : **Harrowden** | Pot : **Potton** | U Cal : **Upper Caldecote** |
| Bro : **Broom** | Hat : **Hatch** | Pul : **Pulloxhill** | U Sto : **Upper Stondon** |
| Cal : **Caldecote** | Hay : **Haynes** | Rad : **Radwell** | Wes : **Westoning** |
| Cam : **Campton** | Hen : **Henlow** | Rav : **Ravensden** | W End : **Wharley End** |
| Car : **Cardington** | Hin : **Hinxworth** | Ren : **Renhold** | Wild : **Wilden** |
| Chic : **Chicksands** | Hol : **Holme** | Rox : **Roxton** | Will : **Willington** |
| Clap : **Clapham** | H Con : **Houghton Conquest** | San : **Sandy** | Wils : **Wilstead** |
| Clif : **Clifton** | Kem : **Kempston** | Shef : **Shefford** | Woo : **Wootton** |
| Clop : **Clophill** | K Har : **Kempston Hardwick** | Shil : **Shillington** | |
| Cop : **Cople** | Lan : **Langford** | Sho : **Shortstown** | |

## A

Abbey Cl. MK41: Ren . . . .2H **7**
    MK42: Els . . . . . . . . . . . . .2B **26**
    MK45: Amp . . . . . . . . . . .3D **40**
Abbey Flds. MK42: Els . . . . . .2B **26**
Abbey Gro. SG19: San . . . . . .3C **20**
Abbey La. MK45: Amp . . . . . .3D **40**
Abbey Rd. MK41: Bed . . . . . .1G **15**
Abbots Wlk. SG18: Big . . . . .3F **31**
    (off High St.)
Abbott Cres. MK42: Kem . . . . .3F **25**
Abrahams Cl.
    MK40: Bed . . . . . . . . . . . . .2E **15**
Acacia Rd. MK42: Bed . . . . . .6D **14**
Acorn Cen. SG18: Big . . . . . .3F **31**
Acorn Cl. MK45: Mau . . . . . . .2D **42**
Acorn Ho. SG18: Big . . . . . . .2E **31**
    (off Sun St.)
Acorn Way MK42: Bed . . . . . .6D **14**

Acres, The SG17: Mep . . . . . . . .5F **45**
Adams Cl. MK42: Kem . . . . . . .4G **25**
    MK45: Amp . . . . . . . . . . .3D **40**
Adamson Ct. MK42: Kem . . . . .6F **13**
    (off Hillgrounds Rd.)
Adamson Wlk. MK42: Kem . . . .6F **13**
    (off Hillgrounds Rd.)
Addington Cl. MK41: Bed . . . . .2G **15**
    SG16: Hen . . . . . . . . . . . .1F **47**
Addingtons Rd.
    MK44: G Bar . . . . . . . . . .4C **10**
Addison Cl. MK42: Kem . . . . .1H **25**
Addison Howard Pk. . . . . . . . .6G **13**
Adelaide Cl. MK45: H Con . . . .5D **28**
Adelaide Sq.
    MK40: Bed . . . . . .2A **52** (2B **14**)
Admiral Row MK45: Flit . . . . . .5C **40**
Aelfric Ct. MK41: Bed . . . . . . .4C **6**
    (off Dearne Wlk.)
Ailesbury Rd. MK45: Amp . . . .2D **40**
Ailwyns Acre MK43: Cran . . . . .5A **32**

Airedale Cl. MK45: Flit . . . . . . .6B **40**
Aire Wlk. MK41: Bed . . . . . . . .2C **6**
Alameda Rd. MK45: Amp . . . . .2C **40**
Alameda Sports Hall . . . . . . . .2B **40**
Alameda Wlk. MK45: Amp . . . .2C **40**
Alamein Av. MK42: Bed . . . . . .5E **15**
Alamein Cl. SG17: Shef . . . . . .1G **45**
Albany Rd.
    MK40: Bed . . . . . . .3D **52** (3C **14**)
Albert Pl. MK45: Amp . . . . . . .4B **40**
Albert Rd. SG15: Arl . . . . . . . .6A **48**
Albert St. MK40: Bed . . .1B **52** (2B **14**)
Albone Way SG18: Big . . . . . . .5E **31**
Albone Way Ind. Est.
    SG18: Big . . . . . . . . . . . . .5E **31**
Alburgh Cl. MK42: Bed . . . . . .6F **15**
Aldenham Cl. MK41: Bed . . . . .3H **15**
Aldens Mead MK42: Bed . . . . . .5F **7**
Alders, The MK42: Kem . . . . . .2G **25**
Aldgate Cl. SG19: Pot . . . . . . .4F **23**

Aldwyck Ct. MK42: Bed . . . . . . .5A **14**
    (off Riverside Cl.)
Alexa Ct. MK42: Bed . . . . . . . . .6G **15**
Alexander Cl.
    MK43: Stew . . . . . . . . . . . .3G **35**
    SG17: Clif . . . . . . . . . . . . .6C **38**
Alexander Rd. SG5: Stot . . . . .4F **49**
Alexander Sports Cen., The . . . .1H **13**
Alexandra Pl.
    MK40: Bed . . . . . . .3A **52** (3A **14**)
Alexandra Rd.
    MK40: Bed . . . . . . .3A **52** (3A **14**)
Alfred Cope Rd. SG19: San . . . .3C **20**
Allen Cl. MK40: Bed . . . . . . . .4H **13**
Allen Ct. MK43: M Mor . . . . . . .3C **34**
Allhallows
    MK40: Bed . . . . . . .3B **52** (3B **14**)
    SG19: San . . . . . . . . . . . .3B **20**
All Saints Rd. MK40: Bed . . . . .3H **13**
    MK44: Cop . . . . . . . . . . . . .4E **17**
All Saints Way SG19: San . . . . .3B **20**

Christie Rd.—Dynes Pl.


Christie Rd. MK42: Bed . . . . . . . .5D 14
Chudleigh Cl. MK40: Bed . . . . . . .1E 15
Church Arc. MK40: Bed . . . . . . . .3B 52
Church Av. MK45: Amp . . . . . . . .1D 40
Church C'way. SG19: Pot . . . . . .4F 23
Church Cl. MK45: H Con . . . . . . .6C 28
MK45: Wes . . . . . . . . . . . . .6B 50
Church Cres. SG18: Lan . . . . . . .1H 39
CHURCH END
Arlesey . . . . . . . . . . . . . .3A 48
Sandy . . . . . . . . . . . . . . .3H 11
Church End MK40: Bid . . . . . . . .3C 12
MK41: Ren . . . . . . . . . . . . .3A 8
MK42: Els . . . . . . . . . . . . .2B 26
MK44: Will . . . . . . . . . . . .2F 17
SG15: Arl . . . . . . . . . . . . .2A 48
Church Farm Av. MK45: Wils . . . .4E 29
Church Farm Cl. SG18: Lan . . . . .1H 39
Churchgate MK44: G Bar . . . . . . .5C 10
Church Hill MK44: Rav . . . . . . . .1G 7
Churchill Cl. MK43: Stew . . . . . .3F 35
Churchill Dr. SG17: Chic . . . . . .4C 36
Churchill Pl. MK44: Will . . . . . . .2F 17
Churchill Rd. MK43: M Mor . . . .4A 34
Churchill Way SG17: Shef . . . . . .6G 37
SG19: San . . . . . . . . . . . . .3C 20
Church La. MK41: Bed . . . . . . . .1H 15
MK43: Brom, Oak . . . . . . . . .2B 4
MK44: Car . . . . . . . . . . . . .6B 16
MK45: F'ton . . . . . . . . . . . .6H 41
SG15: Arl . . . . . . . . . . . . .2A 48
Church M. MK45: Clop . . . . . . .1G 43
Church Path SG19: San . . . . . . .4B 20
Church Rd. MK43: Kem . . . . . . .1C 24
MK43: Woo . . . . . . . . . . . .6A 24
MK44: Will . . . . . . . . . . . .3F 17
MK45: Flit . . . . . . . . . . . . .4A 50
MK45: Mau . . . . . . . . . . . .2H 41
MK45: Pul . . . . . . . . . . . . .4H 51
MK45: Sil . . . . . . . . . . . . .6E 43
MK45: Wes . . . . . . . . . . . .6B 50
MK45: Wils . . . . . . . . . . . .3E 29
SG5: Stot . . . . . . . . . . . . .4F 49
SG16: Hen . . . . . . . . . . . . .6F 39
SG17: Mep . . . . . . . . . . . . .6E 45
Church Row MK43: Woo . . . . . . .6A 24
Church Sq.
MK40: Bed . . . . . . .3B 52 (3B 14)
Church St. MK40: Bed . . .4A 52 (3B 14)
MK45: Amp . . . . . . . . . . . .1D 40
SG17: Clif . . . . . . . . . . . . .6D 38
SG18: Big . . . . . . . . . . . . .3E 31
SG18: Lan . . . . . . . . . . . . .1H 39
SG19: Tem . . . . . . . . . . . . .3H 11
Church Vw. MK41: Clap . . . . . . . .4H 5
MK45: Amp . . . . . . . . . . . .1D 40
Churchville Rd. MK42: Bed . . . . .6B 14
Church Wlk. MK42: Kem . . . . . . .2E 25
(not continuous)
MK43: Cran . . . . . . . . . . . .4A 32
MK43: M Mor . . . . . . . . . . .5B 34
*SG17: Shef . . . . . . . . . . . . .5G 37*
*(off High St.)*
Churnet Cl. MK41: Bed . . . . . . . .2C 6
Cineworld Cinema
Bedford . . . . . . . . . . . . . .4F 15
Clair Ct. MK40: Bed . . . . . . . . . .3B 52
CLAPHAM . . . . . . . . . . . . . . . .3F 5
CLAPHAM GREEN . . . . . . . . . . .3H 5
Clapham Pk. . . . . . . . . . . . . . .2B 6
Clapham Rd.
MK41: Bed, Clap . . . .1A 52 (4H 5)
Claremont Ct. SG18: Big . . . . . .3F 31
Clarendon St.
MK41: Bed . . . . . . .1A 52 (1A 14)
Clare Rd. MK41: Bed . . . . . . . . .4G 7
Claridges La. MK45: Amp . . . . . .1C 40
Claydon Ct.
MK40: Bed . . . . . . .1B 52 (2B 14)
Cleat Hill MK41: Bed . . . . . . . . . .2E 7
Cleeve Abbey MK41: Bed . . . . . .3H 15
Cleveland St. MK42: Kem . . . . . .1G 25
CLIFTON . . . . . . . . . . . . . . . .6C 38
Clifton Farm Barns SG17: Clif . . .5D 38
Clifton Ho. Cl. SG17: Clif . . . . . . .5D 38
Clifton Pk. SG17: Clif . . . . . . . . .1C 46
Clifton Rd. SG16: Hen . . . . . . . .1E 47
SG17: Shef . . . . . . . . . . . . .5H 37
Clipstone Cl. MK41: Bed . . . . . . .6H 7
Cloches, The SG19: Bee . . . . . .6B 20
Cloisters, The MK41: Bed . . . . . .2H 15
MK45: Amp . . . . . . . . . . . . .1D 40
CLOPHILL . . . . . . . . . . . . . . . .2E 43
Clophill Rd. MK45: Grav . . . . . . .5A 44
MK45: Mau . . . . . . . . . . . . .2H 41
Close, The MK41: Clap . . . . . . . . .4G 5
MK44: G Bar . . . . . . . . . . . .4C 10
SG18: Big . . . . . . . . . . . . . .3E 31
Clovelly Way MK40: Bed . . . . . . .1E 15
Clover Av. MK41: Bed . . . . . . . .3H 15
Clover Cl. SG18: Big . . . . . . . . . .5H 31
Clover Rd. MK45: Flit . . . . . . . . . .2B 50
Club Rd. MK45: Wils . . . . . . . . . .4E 29
Cluny Way SG15: Arl . . . . . . . . . .5A 48
Clyde Cres. MK41: Bed . . . . . . . . .4D 6
Coach Rd. SG16: Hen . . . . . . . . .1F 47
Cobbett La. MK45: F'ton . . . . . . .6A 42
Cobbitts Rd. MK45: Mau . . . . . . .1G 41
Cobden Sq.
MK40: Bed . . . . . . .1B 52 (2B 14)
Cody Rd. MK41: Clap . . . . . . . . . .3G 5
Colchester Way MK41: Bed . . . . . .4G 7
Coles Cl. MK41: Bed . . . . . . . . . .2G 15
College Ct. MK42: Kem . . . . . . . .1A 26
College Rd. MK42: Bed . . . . . . . .6B 14
SG19: San . . . . . . . . . . . . . .2C 20
College St. MK42: Kem . . . . . . . .1A 26
Collie Rd. MK42: Bed . . . . . . . . .5E 15
Collins Pl. MK42: Bed . . . . . . . . .6F 15
Coltsfoot SG18: Big . . . . . . . . . .5H 31
Columbine Cl. MK41: Bed . . . . . . .5A 8
Comet Dr. MK42: Sho . . . . . . . . .3G 27
Commerce Way MK45: Flit . . . . . .6E 41
Commercial Rd.
MK40: Bed . . . . . . .4A 52 (3B 14)
Common Farm La.
MK45: Flit . . . . . . . . . . . . . .6B 40
Common Rd. SG5: Stot . . . . . . . .2F 49
SG18: Lan . . . . . . . . . . . . . .4G 39
SG19: Pot . . . . . . . . . . . . . .3E 23
Compass Dr. MK42: Sho . . . . . . .2G 27
Compton Cl. MK45: Flit . . . . . . . .3B 50
Concorde Cl. MK42: Sho . . . . . . .3G 27
Conduit Rd. MK40: Bed . . . . . . . .2A 14
Coneygate SG17: Mep . . . . . . . . .5F 45
Coniston Cl. MK42: Kem . . . . . . .1G 25
Coniston Rd. MK45: Flit . . . . . . . .2C 50
Connaught Way MK41: Bed . . . . . .3D 6
Conquest Rd. MK42: Bed . . . . . . .6C 14
Constable Hill MK41: Bed . . . . . .1A 14
Conway Cres. MK41: Bed . . . . . . .4C 6
Conway Dr. MK45: Flit . . . . . . . . .3B 50
Cooks Way SG18: Big . . . . . . . . .3G 31
Coombs Cl. MK42: Bed . . . . . . . .5D 14
Coopers Cl. MK40: Bid . . . . . . . .3E 13
MK44: G Bar . . . . . . . . . . . .4A 10
SG18: Big . . . . . . . . . . . . . .5G 31
SG19: San . . . . . . . . . . . . . .5B 20
Coopers Ct. SG17: Shef . . . . . . . .6H 37
Copelands SG18: Big . . . . . . . . .3F 31
Copeland Wlk. MK41: Bed . . . . . .6H 7
COPLE . . . . . . . . . . . . . . . . . .5E 17
Cople Rd. MK44: Car . . . . . . . . . .6C 16
Coppens, The SG5: Stot . . . . . . .5G 49
Coppice Mead SG5: Stot . . . . . . .5E 49
SG18: Big . . . . . . . . . . . . . .4G 31
Coppins, The MK45: Amp . . . . . .2D 40
Copse, The MK41: Bed . . . . . . . .1H 15
Copthorne Cl. MK43: Oak . . . . . . .1C 4
Corby Cl. MK42: Bed . . . . . . . . .1D 26
Corfe Rd. MK41: Bed . . . . . . . . . .5G 7
Cornish Cl. SG17: Shef . . . . . . . .5G 37
Cornland MK41: Bed . . . . . . . . . .6G 7
Cornwallis Cl. MK43: Brom . . . . . .6A 4
Cornwall Rd. MK40: Bed . . . . . . .1D 14
MK45: Amp . . . . . . . . . . . . .2D 40
Coronation Rd. MK43: Cran . . . . .3B 32
Cosmic Av. MK42: Bed . . . . . . . .1A 26
Costin St. MK40: Bed . . .4A 52 (3B 14)
Cotman Cl. MK41: Bed . . . . . . . . .6B 6
Cotswold Cl. MK41: Bed . . . . . . . .6F 7
Cotswold Pl. MK45: Flit . . . . . . . .2B 50
Cottage Rd. SG19: San . . . . . . . .2B 20
Cotton End Rd. MK45: Wils . . . . .3F 29
Cottril Way MK42: Bed . . . . . . . .5E 15
Countess Gdns.
MK42: Kem . . . . . . . . . . . . .2F 25
Courtlands Dr. SG18: Big . . . . . . .6H 31
Court Rd. MK43: Cran . . . . . . . . .3B 32
Coventry Rd. MK40: Bed . . . . . . .3H 13
Cow Cl. SG18: Hol . . . . . . . . . . .6F 31
Cowper Rd. MK40: Bed . . . . . . . .1H 13
Cox's Cl. MK40: Bed . . . . . . . . . .4H 13
Cox's Way SG15: Arl . . . . . . . . . .4A 48
Crab La. SG18: Big . . . . . . . . . . .3F 31
(not continuous)
Crackle Hill Rd. SG17: Mep . . . .4G 45
Cranborne Cl. MK41: Bed . . . . . . .5H 7
Crancott Cl. MK45: H Con . . . . . .5D 28
Crane Way MK43: Cran . . . . . . . .2C 32
CRANFIELD . . . . . . . . . . . . . . .2B 32
Cranfield University
Silsoe Campus . . . . . . . . . .6E 43
Crawley Rd. MK43: Cran . . . . . . .1A 32
Crayton Rd. MK45: Amp . . . . . . .2C 40
Crediton Cl. MK40: Bed . . . . . . . .1E 15
Crescent, The
MK40: Bed . . . . . . .2A 52 (2B 14)
MK42: Sho . . . . . . . . . . . . .2G 27
MK43: Stew . . . . . . . . . . . . .3G 35
MK44: Mog . . . . . . . . . . . . .4E 19
MK45: Amp . . . . . . . . . . . . .3B 40
SG16: Hen . . . . . . . . . . . . . .6E 47
SG18: Stan . . . . . . . . . . . . .1C 38
SG19: Bee . . . . . . . . . . . . . .6B 20
Crescent Ct. MK40: Bed . . . . . . . .1A 52
Cricket Cl. MK41: Bed . . . . . . . .1G 15
Cricketer's Rd. SG15: Arl . . . . . . .6A 48
Cricket La. MK41: Bed . . . . . . . .1G 15
Croft, The MK41: Bed . . . . . . . . .1G 15
MK45: Flit . . . . . . . . . . . . . .1C 50
Crofton Cl. MK41: Bed . . . . . . . . .5D 6
Crofts, The SG5: Stot . . . . . . . . .4F 49
Cromwell Ct. *MK42: Kem . . . . . .1G 25*
*(off Farrer St.)*
Cromwell Rd. MK40: Bed . . . . . . .4H 13
Cross St. MK40: Bed . . . .2B 52 (2B 14)
Crossways Cl. SG16: Hen . . . . . .1F 47
Crowe Rd. MK40: Bed . . . . . . . . .3H 13
Crow Hill SG19: San . . . . . . . . . .1A 20
Crown La. SG18: Lan . . . . . . . . . .2H 39
Crown Lodge SG15: Arl . . . . . . . .6A 48
Crown Pl. MK42: Bed . . .6A 52 (4B 14)
Crown Quay
MK40: Bed . . . . . . .5A 52 (4B 14)
Crowther Ct. SG18: Big . . . . . . . .2E 31
Croxden Way MK42: Els . . . . . . . .2C 26
Croyland Dr. MK42: Els . . . . . . . .2D 26
Cryselco Cl. MK42: Kem . . . . . . .2F 25
Cuckoo Cl. SG19: San . . . . . . . . .1B 20
Culver Ho. *MK40: Bed . . . . . . . .1A 14*
*(off Linden Rd.)*
Curlew Cres. MK41: Bed . . . . . . . .5B 6
Cutcliffe Gdns. MK40: Bed . . . . .3H 13
Cutcliffe Gro. MK40: Bed . . . . . . .2H 13
Cutcliffe Pl. MK40: Bed . . . . . . . .3H 13
Cut Throat La. MK41: Bed . . . . . .1H 13
Cynthia Ct. MK43: Woo . . . . . . . .6C 24


## D


Dahl Cl. MK42: Bed . . . . . . . . . .1C 26
Dairy, The SG16: Hen . . . . . . . . .1F 47
Dale Cl. MK41: Bed . . . . . . . . . . .6G 7
Dallas Rd. MK42: Bed . . . . . . . . .5A 14
Dame Alice Ct.
MK40: Bed . . . . . . .3D 52 (3C 14)
Dame Alice St.
MK40: Bed . . . . . . .2B 52 (2B 14)
Dane Cl. SG5: Stot . . . . . . . . . . .2F 49
Dane La. MK45: Wils . . . . . . . . . .2C 28
Dane St. MK40: Bed . . . .3B 52 (3B 14)
Dapifer Dr. SG19: San . . . . . . . .3C 20
Dark La. SG18: Big . . . . . . . . . . .3E 31
Darlington Cl. SG19: San . . . . . . .2D 20
Darlow Dr. MK40: Bid . . . . . . . . .3F 13
Dart Rd. MK41: Bed . . . . . . . . . . .4C 6
Darwin Rd. MK42: Bed . . . . . . . .6C 14
Davis Cl. MK42: Bed . . . . . . . . . .6C 14
Davis Row SG15: Arl . . . . . . . . . .6A 48
Dawlish Dr. MK40: Bed . . . . . . . .2E 15
Dawson Cl. SG16: Hen . . . . . . . . .5E 47
Daysfield MK45: H Con . . . . . . . .5D 28
Day's La. MK40: Bid . . . . . . . . . .2E 13
Deacon Av. MK42: Kem . . . . . . . .3E 25
Deacon M. MK43: M Mor . . . . . . .4A 34
Dean St. MK40: Bed . . . . . . . . . .2F 15
Dearmans Cl. MK45: Clop . . . . . .1E 43
Dearne Wlk. MK41: Bed . . . . . . . .4C 6
DEEPDALE . . . . . . . . . . . . . . . .4B 22
Deep Spinney MK40: Bid . . . . . . .2D 12
Deeside MK41: Bed . . . . . . . . . . .4D 6
De Havilland Av. MK42: Sho . . . .3G 27
Delamare Cl. SG19: San . . . . . . .2B 20
Delamere Wlk. MK41: Bed . . . . . .6H 7
Dell, The MK42: Kem . . . . . . . . .3D 24
Dells, The SG18: Big . . . . . . . . . .4F 31
Dells La. SG18: Big . . . . . . . . . . .4F 31
De Montfort University
Polhill Campus . . . . . . . . . .1F 15
Lansdowne Campus
. . . . . . . . . . . . . .1A 52 (2A 14)
Denbigh Cl. MK43: M Mor . . . . . .4B 34
Denbigh Way MK41: Bed . . . . . . . .5G 7
Denel Cl. MK45: Flit . . . . . . . . . .6C 40
Dene Way SG18: U Cal . . . . . . . .1A 30
Denmark St. MK40: Bed . . . . . . .2E 15
Dennis Cl. MK41: Clap . . . . . . . . .2E 5
Dennis Ct. MK42: Kem . . . . . . . .3F 25
Dennis Rd. MK42: Kem . . . . . . . .3E 25
Denton Cl. MK42: Kem . . . . . . . . .5F 13
Denton Dr. MK43: M Mor . . . . . . .4A 34
Dents Rd. MK42: Bed . . . . . . . . .5D 14
De Parys Av.
MK40: Bed . . . . . . .1C 52 (1C 14)
De Parys Lodge MK40: Bed . . . . .2B 52
Derby Pl. MK40: Bed . . . . . . . . .1B 52
Derwent Av. SG18: Big . . . . . . . .5G 31
Derwent Pl. MK42: Bed . . . . . . . .5B 14
Derwent Ri. MK45: Flit . . . . . . . .2B 50
Derwent Rd. SG16: Hen . . . . . . .6D 46
Devizes Av. MK41: Bed . . . . . . . . .4G 7
Devon Rd. MK40: Bed . . . . . . . . .2D 14
Dewlands MK43: Oak . . . . . . . . . .2B 4
Dew Pond Rd. MK45: Flit . . . . . . .3B 50
Dickens Ct. SG18: Big . . . . . . . . .4F 31
Dickens Rd. MK45: Flit . . . . . . . .1A 50
Digswell Cl. SG17: Shef . . . . . . .6H 37
Dimmock Rd. MK43: Woo . . . . . .6B 24
Dines Cl. MK45: Wils . . . . . . . . .3E 29
Ditmas Av. MK42: Kem . . . . . . . .3D 24
Donnelly Dr. MK41: Bed . . . . . . .2G 15
Doolittle Mill MK45: Amp . . . . . .5B 40
Dorchester Way MK42: Els . . . . .2C 26
Dorsey Dr. MK42: Bed . . . . . . . .6B 14
Dothans Cl. MK44: G Bar . . . . . . .4B 10
Doug Harris Way MK45: Sil . . . . .6D 42
Douglas Rd. MK41: Bed . . . . . . . .3D 6
Dove Cl. SG19: San . . . . . . . . . .1C 20
Dovehouse Cl.
MK43: Brom . . . . . . . . . . . . .1B 12
Dove Ho. Dr. SG16: Hen . . . . . . .1F 47
Dover Cres. MK41: Bed . . . . . . . . .4G 7
Dove Rd. MK41: Bed . . . . . . . . . .5D 6
Dove Wlk. MK45: Flit . . . . . . . . .3C 50
Downfield Way MK42: Kem . . . . .6G 13
Downside MK41: Bed . . . . . . . . . .6G 7
Downside Gdns. SG19: Pot . . . . .3E 23
Dragons Health Club
Bedford . . . . . . . . . . . . . . .6D 6
Drapers End MK43: M Mor . . . . .5A 34
Drayton Rd. MK42: Kem . . . . . . .3F 25
Drive, The MK43: Oak . . . . . . . . .2B 4
Drove Rd. SG18: Big . . . . . . . . .2G 31
Duchess Rd. MK42: Bed . . . . . . .1F 27
DUCK END
Maulden . . . . . . . . . . . . . .2F 41
Wilstead . . . . . . . . . . . . . .2E 29
Duck End Cl. MK45: H Con . . . . .6A 28
Duck End La. MK40: Bid . . . . . . .2D 12
MK45: Mau . . . . . . . . . . . . .2F 41
MK45: Wils . . . . . . . . . . . . .2E 29
Duck La. *SG17: Shef . . . . . . . . .5G 37*
*(off High St.)*
Duckmill Cres.
MK42: Bed . . . . . . .4D 52 (3C 14)
Duckmill La.
MK42: Bed . . . . . . .5C 52 (4C 14)
Duck Mill Wlk.
MK40: Bed . . . . . . .4C 52 (3C 14)
Dudley Cl. MK42: Kem . . . . . . . .2G 25
Dudley St. MK40: Bed . . . . . . . . .2E 15
Duke Dr. MK41: Clap . . . . . . . . . .2F 5
Dukes Ct. MK45: Flit . . . . . . . . .2E 51
Dukes Rd. MK45: Amp . . . . . . . .2D 40
Duke St. MK40: Bed . . .3C 52 (3C 14)
Duncombe St. MK42: Kem . . . . . .1H 25
Dunham Cl. MK42: Bed . . . . . . . .6F 15
Dunkirk Cl. MK42: Kem . . . . . . .6A 14
Dunstable Cl. MK45: Flit . . . . . . .2C 50
Dunstable Rd. MK45: Flit . . . . . . .3C 50
Dunstable St. MK45: Amp . . . . . .3C 40
Dunster Gdns. MK41: Bed . . . . . . .4H 7
Dunton La. SG18: Big . . . . . . . . .5H 31
(not continuous)
Dunvegan Way MK41: Bed . . . . . . .4F 7
Dunville Rd. MK40: Bed . . . . . . .3H 13
Durham Cl. MK45: Flit . . . . . . . .6C 40
SG18: Big . . . . . . . . . . . . . .5F 31
Durler Av. MK42: Kem . . . . . . . .3D 24
Dynes Pl. MK44: Mog . . . . . . . . .4E 19


56 A-Z Bedford

**Grn. End Rd.** MK43: Kem 2B 24
MK44: G Bar 3A 10
**GREENFIELD** 2G 51
**Greenfield Rd.** MK45: Flit 2E 51
MK45: F'ton 1H 51
MK45: Pul 2H 51
MK45: Wes 6C 50
**Greenhill St.**
MK40: Bed 3A 52 (3B 14)
**Grn. Keepers Rd.**
MK40: Bid 5D 12
**Green La.** MK41: Clap 4G 5
MK41: Ren 3H 7
MK43: Stew 3F 35
SG19: Eve 1A 22
**Greens Cl.** SG19: San 4C 20
**Greenshields Rd.** MK40: Bed 3E 15
**Greenview Cl.** MK42: Kem 2E 25
**Green Way** SG17: Cam 1E 45
**Greenways** MK45: Flit 1D 50
**Gregory Cl.** SG17: Mep 5F 45
**Grenidge Way** MK43: Oak 1B 4
**Gresham Way** SG17: Shef 4G 37
**Greskine Cl.** MK41: Bed 5A 8
**Greycote** MK42: Sho 2G 27
**Greyfriars** MK40: Bed 2A 52 (2A 14)
(not continuous)
**Greystoke Wlk.** MK41: Bed 5F 7
**Grieg Cl.** SG17: Shef 5H 37
**Grisedale Ct.** MK42: Kem 3G 25
**Grosvenor Ct.** *MK40: Bed 3A 14*
*(off The Avenue)*
**Grosvenor Gdns.** SG18: Big 3G 31
**Grosvenor St.** MK42: Bed 5C 14
**Grove, The**
MK40: Bed 2D 52 (2C 14)
MK45: H Con 6C 28
MK45: Sil 5D 42
MK45: Wes 6B 50
SG18: Big 4G 31
**Grovebury Ct.** MK43: Woo 6B 24
**Grove Ct.** SG15: Arl 3A 48
**Groveland Way** SG5: Stot 5G 49
**Grove Pl.** MK40: Bed 3D 52 (3C 14)
**Groveside** SG16: Hen 6F 39
**Guinness Pl.** MK41: Bed 3G 15
**Gulliver Cl.** MK42: Kem 6F 13
**Gunnersbury Pk.** MK41: Bed 2H 15
**Gurneys La.** SG18: Lan 1H 39
**Guru Ravidass La.**
MK40: Bed 3A 14
**Gwyn Ct.** MK40: Bed 3A 52
**Gwyn St.** MK40: Bed 2A 52 (2B 14)
**Gypsy La.** SG18: Big, Bro 6C 30

## H

**Haden Cl.** MK41: Bed 6A 6
**Hadfield Ct.** MK42: Bed 5B 14
**Hadleigh Cl.** MK41: Bed 5G 7
**Hailes Cl.** MK41: Bed 4E 7
**Halegate** MK43: Woo 5B 24
**Hale Lodge** MK40: Bed 1C 14
**Halesowen Dr.** MK42: Els 2D 26
**Halifax Rd.** MK42: Sho 3G 27
**HALL END**
**MK43** 5A 24
**MK45** 2D 42
**Hall End Cl.** MK45: Mau 2D 42
**Hall End Rd.** MK43: Woo 4A 24
**Hallworth Dr.** SG5: Stot 4E 49
**Hallworth Ho.** *SG5: Stot 4E 49*
*(off Hallworth Dr.)*
**Halsey Rd.** MK42: Kem 6G 13
**Hamble Rd.** MK41: Bed 2D 6
**Hammond Rd.** MK41: Bed 5A 8
**Hampden Cl.** MK45: Flit 3C 50
**Hampden Ct.** MK40: Bid 2D 12
**Hampden Rd.** MK45: Flit 3C 50
**Hampton Cl.** MK45: Wils 3F 29
**Hamsterley Cl.** MK41: Bed 5H 7
**Handley Ct.** *SG19: San 2B 20*
*(off Bunyan Rd.)*
**Hanover Ct.** MK40: Bed 1A 14
MK43: Woo 5B 24
**Harbrook La.** SG17: Clif 6C 38
**Harding Cl.** MK42: Bed 5D 14
**Hardwick Cl.** SG17: Shef 5G 37
**Hardwick Hill** MK45: K Har 6H 25
**Hardwick Rd.** MK42: Bed 5C 14
**Harefield Av.** MK42: Bed 1A 26
**Harewood Rd.** MK42: Bed 1C 26
**Hargreaves Ct.** MK42: Bed 1C 26
**Harlech Rd.** MK41: Bed 5F 7
**Harpenden Cl.** MK41: Bed 2G 15
**Harpur Cen.**
MK40: Bed 3B 52 (3B 14)
**Harpur Ho.** MK42: Bed 5D 52
**Harpur Sq.**
MK40: Bed 3B 52 (3B 14)
**Harpur St.** MK40: Bed 3B 52 (2B 14)
**Harrier Cl.** SG18: Big 5E 31
**Harrier Mill** SG16: Hen 5E 39
**Harriers, The** SG19: San 2B 20
**Harrier Way** MK42: Kem 3G 25
**Harrington Dr.** MK41: Bed 4E 7
**Harris Cl.** MK42: Kem 1G 25
**Harrold Priory** MK41: Bed 3H 15
**HARROWDEN** 2F 27
**Harrowden La.** MK42: Bed 1E 27
MK42: Har 2G 27
MK44: Car 6A 16
**Harrowden Rd.** MK42: Bed 1E 27
(not continuous)
**Harrow Piece** MK45: Mau 1G 41
**Harter Av.** MK43: Cran 5A 32
**Harter Rd.** MK42: Kem 2F 25
**Hartington St.** MK41: Bed 1B 14
**Hartland Av.** MK40: Bed 2E 15
**Hartop Cl.** MK41: Bed 5F 7
**Hartshill** MK41: Bed 6E 7
**Hartwell Dr.** MK42: Kem 5G 13
**Harvey Cl.** SG18: U Cal 1B 30
**Harvey Rd.** MK41: Bed 1G 15
**Hassett St.**
MK40: Bed 3A 52 (3B 14)
**Hastings Rd.** MK42: Kem 3F 25
**HATCH** 6H 19
**Hatfield Av.** MK43: Cran 5B 32
**Hatfield Cl.** MK45: Flit 1D 50
**Hatfield Cres.** MK41: Bed 2F 15
MK45: Flit 1D 50
**Hatfield Rd.** MK45: Flit 1D 50
**Hatley Rd.** SG19: Pot 4F 23
**Havelock Cl.** SG19: San 2B 20
**Havelock Rd.** SG18: Big 2F 31
**Havelock St.** MK40: Bed 4A 14
**Haven, The** SG5: Stot 4F 49
**Hawes Cl.** MK45: Flit 1C 50
**Hawes Ct.** MK40: Bed 3B 52 (3B 14)
**Hawesmere Cl.** SG18: Big 5F 31
**Hawk Cl.** MK45: Flit 2B 50
**Hawk Dr.** MK41: Bed, Clap 3B 6
SG19: San 1B 20
**Hawkins Rd.** MK42: Bed 6C 14
**Hawthorn Cl.** MK45: Amp 3D 40
SG18: Big 1E 31
**Hawthorne Av.** MK40: Bed 4G 13
**Hawthorne Cl.** MK45: Clop 1G 43
**Hawthorne Dr.** MK45: Wils 4E 29
**Hawthorns, The** MK43: Cran 3B 32
MK45: Flit 1C 50
SG16: Hen 5F 39
**Hawthorn Ter.** MK43: Brom 1A 12
**Hawthorn Way** MK45: Sil 6D 42
**Haycroft** MK43: Woo 6C 24
**Haylands Way** MK41: Bed 1F 15
**Haylock Cl.** MK42: Kem 3E 25
**Haynes Rd.** MK42: Bed 6C 14
**Hazel Cl.** SG17: Shef 6F 37
**Hazel Gro.** SG5: Stot 5E 49
**Hazel Wlk.** SG18: Big 1E 31
**Hazelwood Rd.** MK42: Bed 6D 14
**Heather Dr.** SG18: Big 5H 31
**Heather Gdns.** MK41: Bed 2H 15
**Heathfield** MK41: Bed 6G 7
**Hedley Way** MK45: Mau 2D 42
**Helford Cl.** MK41: Bed 3D 6
**Helmsley Av.** MK41: Bed 4G 7
**Henderson Way** MK42: Kem 1H 25
**Henley Rd.** MK40: Bed 3A 14
**HENLOW** 6F 39
**Henlow Greyhound Stadium** 6C 46
**Henlow Ind. Est.** SG16: Hen 6D 46
**Herbrand Rd.** MK42: Bed 1F 27
**Hereford Gro.** SG18: Big 5F 31
**Hereford Rd.** MK42: Bed 1E 27
**Hermitage, The** SG15: Arl 2B 48
**Heron Cl.** SG17: Shef 6G 37
SG18: Big 5E 31
SG19: San 5B 20
**Heron Hgts.** *MK41: Bed 1G 15*
*(off Goldington Grn.)*
**Heron Quay**
MK40: Bed 4A 52 (3B 14)
**Heron Rd.** MK45: Flit 3C 50
**Heronscroft** MK41: Bed 6F 7
**Herons Mead** MK43: Brom 1B 12
**Heron Way** SG5: Stot 4E 49
**Hiam Bus. Cen.** MK45: Mau 4H 41
**Hickling Cl.** MK40: Bed 4G 13
**Higham Bury** MK45: Pul 6G 51
**Highbury Gro.** MK41: Clap 2F 5
**Highbush Rd.** SG5: Stot 5E 49
**Highfield Rd.** MK42: Kem 2G 25
MK43: Oak 1C 4
MK45: F'ton 6A 42
**Highfields** MK45: Wes 6C 50
**Highfields Ct.** MK45: Wes 5C 50
**Highlands** MK45: Flit 1C 50
**High Rd.** SG18: Bro 6B 30
SG19: Bee 5B 20
**High Rd., The**
MK42: Bed, Har 1G 27
**High St.** MK40: Bed 3C 52 (3C 14)
MK41: Clap 3F 5
MK42: Els 1B 26
MK42: Kem 2E 25
MK43: Cran 4A 32
MK43: Oak 1B 4
MK44: Blun 6G 11
MK44: G Bar 4B 10
MK44: Rox 1G 11
MK45: Clop 2E 43
MK45: Flit 6C 40
MK45: F'ton 6H 41
MK45: Grav 6A 44
MK45: Gre 3F 51
MK45: H Con 5D 28
MK45: Sil 5E 43
MK45: Wes 6C 50
SG5: Stot 4E 49
SG15: Arl 4A 48
SG16: Hen 1F 47
SG17: Mep 5F 45
SG17: Shef 5G 37
SG18: Big 3E 31
SG18: Bro 6B 30
SG18: Lan 3G 39
SG19: San 4C 20
**High Vw.** MK41: Bed 6G 7
**Highway, The** MK42: Har, Sho 2G 27
**Hilbre Grange** MK40: Bed 1A 14
**Hill, The** MK44: Blun 6F 11
**Hillary Ri.** SG15: Arl 5B 48
**Hillcrest** MK43: Cran 2C 32
**Hilldene Cl.** MK45: Flit 1C 50
**Hillesden Av.** MK42: Els 1B 26
**Hillgrounds Rd.** MK42: Kem 5F 13
**Hillier Ct.** MK40: Bed 2A 52
**Hill La.** SG18: Big, U Cal 3A 30
**Hill La. Crossroads**
SG18: O War 3A 30
**Hill Plantation** *MK43: Brom 2A 12*
*(off Brookside Mobile Home Pk.)*
**Hill Ri.** MK41: Bed 6B 6
MK42: Kem 3D 24
**Hills Cl.** MK44: Rox 2G 11
**Hillson Cl.** MK43: M Mor 4B 34
**Hilltop Vw.** SG17: Mep 4F 45
**Hill Vw.** SG19: Bee 6C 20
**Hindburn Cl.** MK41: Bed 3D 6
**Hinksley Rd.** MK45: Flit 1C 50
**Hinwick Cl.** SG15: Arl 3B 48
**Hinxworth Rd.** SG7: Hin 1H 49
**Hitchin La.** SG17: Clif 6D 38
**Hitchin Rd.** SG5: Stot 6D 48
SG15: Arl 6A 48
SG16: Hen 6D 46
SG17: Shef 6H 37
SG18: U Cal 2A 30
**Hitchin St.** SG18: Big 4E 31
**Hitchmead Rd.** SG18: Big 3G 31
**Hockley Ct.** MK43: M Mor 4B 34
**Hockliffe Rd.** MK42: Bed 5D 14
**Hodder Rd.** MK41: Bed 2C 6
**Hogarth Cl.** MK41: Bed 1B 14
**Holden Cl.** MK40: Bid 2D 12
**Holland Rd.** MK45: Amp 3B 40
**Hollies, The** MK42: Kem 2H 25
SG17: Shef 5G 37
**Hollies Wlk.** MK43: Woo 5B 24
**Hollybush Rd.** MK45: Flit 2D 50
**Holly Cl.** SG18: Big 1F 31
**Holly Wlk.** MK45: Sil 6D 42
**HOLME** 6E 31
**Holme Cl.** MK43: M Mor 4B 34
**Holme Ct. Av.** SG18: Big 5G 31
**Holme Cres.** SG18: Big 4F 31
**Holme Mills** SG18: Hol 6E 31
**Holme St.** MK42: Bed 6B 52 (4B 14)
**Holmewood Rd.** MK45: Gre 2H 51
**Holt Row** MK42: Bed 6B 52 (4B 14)
**Holywell Rd.** MK43: Cran 3C 32
**Homebrook Ho.**
MK42: Bed 5C 52 (4C 14)
**Home Cl.** MK41: Ren 3H 7
MK45: H Con 5C 28
MK45: Wils 4E 29
SG5: Stot 4F 49
**Home Farm Way** MK45: Wes 6C 50
**Home Rd.** MK43: Kem 2B 24
**Honey Hill Gdns.** MK40: Bed 4G 13
**Honey Hill Rd.** MK40: Bed 4G 13
**Honeysuckle Av.** MK45: Wils 5E 29
**Honeysuckle Cl.** SG18: Big 5H 31
**Honeysuckle Way** MK41: Bed 2H 15
**Honiton Way** MK40: Bed 1E 15
**Hoo, The** MK42: Kem 3D 24
**Hoo Cl.** MK43: Woo 5B 24
**Hoo Hill Maze** 1A 46
**Hooked La.** MK45: Wils 2G 29
**Hookhams La.** MK41: Ren 4H 7
**Hoo La.** MK43: Woo 1C 34
**Hooper Cl.** MK42: Kem 3E 25
**Hoo Rd.** SG17: Mep 4G 45
**Hoover Pl.** SG17: Chic 6C 36
**Hope Rd.** MK42: Bed 1B 26
**Hornbeams, The** MK42: Kem 1H 25
**Horne La.** MK40: Bed 4B 52 (3B 14)
SG19: Pot 4E 23
**Horner Gro.** MK43: Brom 5C 4
**Hornes End Rd.** MK45: Flit 3C 50
**Horseshoe, The** MK42: Bed 6B 52
**Horseshoe Cl.** MK43: M Mor 3C 34
**Horseshoe Ct.** *MK42: Kem 2F 25*
*(off Bedford Rd.)*
**Horslow St.** SG19: Pot 4E 23
**Hospital Rd.** SG15: Arl 6H 47
**Hotch Cft.** MK43: Cran 1C 32
**Houghton Cl.** MK45: Amp 3C 40
**HOUGHTON CONQUEST** 5D 28
**Houghton Rd.** MK42: Bed 5B 14
**House La.** SG15: Arl 3A 48
**Howard Av.** MK40: Bed 3H 13
**Howard Cen.**
MK40: Bed 4B 52 (3B 14)
**Howard Cl.** MK44: Car 6C 16
MK45: Wils 4E 29
SG5: Stot 5E 49
**Howard Ct.** MK45: Flit 3C 50
**Howard Pl.** MK40: Bed 3H 13
**Howards M.** MK45: Clop 2E 43
**Howard St.**
MK40: Bed 3C 52 (3C 14)
MK42: Kem 1H 25
**Howberry Grn.** SG15: Arl 6H 47
**Howbury Hall** MK41: Ren 5D 8
**Howbury Hall Est.** MK41: Ren 5D 8
**Howbury St.** MK40: Bed 2D 14
**Howden Gdns.** MK40: Bid 2E 13
**Howes Dr.** MK43: M Mor 5A 34
**Howes La.** MK45: Wes 6C 50
**Howkin Cl.** MK43: Brom 1A 12
**Hubbard Cl.** MK45: Flit 3C 50
**Huddleston Way** MK41: Bed 3G 15
**Hudson Rd.** MK41: Bed 6A 8
**Hulme Cl.** MK41: Clap 2E 5
MK42: Kem 1G 25
**Humber Av.** MK41: Bed 4D 6
**Hunter Cl.** MK42: Sho 3F 27
**Hunters Cl.** MK41: Clap 3E 5
SG5: Stot 4E 49
**Huntingdon Rd.** MK42: Kem 2F 25
**Hunts Fld.** MK44: G Bar 4B 10
**Hunts Path** MK43: Oak 1C 4
**Hurst Gro.** MK40: Bed 3H 13
**Hyde Av.** SG5: Stot 5E 49
**Hyde Cl.** SG17: Shef 6A 38

## I

**Ibbett Cl.** MK43: Kem 2C 24
**Ibbett La.** SG19: Pot 4D 22
**Ickwell Rd.** SG18: U Cal 1A 30
**Iddesleigh Rd.** MK40: Bed 4H 13
**Ingram Cl.** MK43: M Mor 4A 34
**Inns La.** MK45: Sil 6D 42
**Interchange Retail Pk.**
MK42: Kem 3H 25

Manor Rd.—Old Vicarage Gdns.

**Manor Rd.** MK43: K Har 6E **25**
MK43: M Mor 5A **34**
MK43: Woo 6C **24**
SG16: Hen 1E **47**
SG19: San 3B **20**
**Manor Way** MK45: Flit 3B **50**
SG19: Pot 3F **23**
**Manton Cen.** MK41: Bed 6A **6**
**Manton Cen., The** MK41: Bed 6A **6**
**Manton Cl.** MK45: Amp 2D **40**
**Manton Ind. Est.** MK41: Bed 5A **6**
**Manton La.** MK41: Bed 5A **6**
**Maple Cl.** MK45: Pul 2H **51**
MK45: Wils 4F **29**
SG17: Clif 6B **38**
SG18: Big 2F **31**
**Maple Dr.** SG17: Shef 6A **38**
**Maple Rd.** SG19: San 2C **20**
**Maples, The** *MK42: Kem 2G 25*
*(off Bunyan Rd.)*
MK42: Kem 2G **25**
(The Links)
MK45: Sil 6D **42**
**Maple Way** MK43: Cran 4A **32**
**Mardale Cl.** MK42: Kem 1G **25**
**Maresfield Av.** SG17: Chic 6D **36**
**Mareth Rd.** MK42: Bed 5E **15**
**Margetts Rd.** MK42: Kem 1H **25**
**Marigold Way** MK42: Bed 1E **27**
**Marina Ct.** MK42: Bed 5A **14**
**Market Sq.** SG18: Big 3F **31**
SG19: Pot 4E **23**
SG19: San 4C **20**
(not continuous)
**Mark Rutherford Rd.**
MK42: Bed 5D **14**
**Marlborough Pk.** MK42: Kem 5H **13**
**Marlborough Rd.** MK40: Bed 3H **13**
**Marlow Way** MK41: Bed 3C **6**
**Marne St.** MK42: Kem 6A **14**
**Marschefield** SG5: Stot 4E **49**
**Marshall Cl.** MK42: Kem 6F **13**
**Marshall Ct.** MK41: Bed 2G **15**
**Marsh Leys** MK43: Kem 5F **25**
**Marston Hill** MK43: M Mor 2E **33**
**MARSTON MORETAINE** **4B 34**
**Marston Vale Millennium Country Pk.** **3C 34**
**Martham Cl.** MK40: Bed 4F **13**
**Martin Cl.** MK41: Bed 5D **6**
**Martin Rd.** MK45: Flit 3B **50**
**Maryville Rd.** MK42: Bed 6B **14**
**Marywells** SG17: Mep 5F **45**
**Massey Cl.** MK42: Kem 1G **25**
**MAULDEN** **2H 41**
**Maulden Rd.** MK45: Flit 2E **51**
**Maulden Rd. Ind. Est.**
MK45: Flit 6E **41**
**Mayfield Cl.** MK42: Kem 6G **13**
**Mayfield Ct.** SG19: San 4B **20**
**Mayfields** SG17: Shef 5H **37**
**Mayhew Ct.** MK43: Brom 2A **12**
**Maynards, The** SG18: Bro 6B **30**
**Mayston Cl.** SG19: Pot 4C **22**
**Mead End** SG18: Big 4G **31**
**Meadow Cl.** SG19: Bee 6B **20**
**Meadow La.** MK44: Car 4B **16**
**Meadows, The** MK43: Stew 3G **35**
MK45: Flit 5B **40**
**Meadowsweet Dr.** MK42: Bed 1E **27**
**Meadowview Rd.** MK42: Kem 2E **25**
**Meadow Wlk.** SG16: Hen 1F **47**
**Meadow Way** MK45: Amp 3B **40**
SG5: Stot 4F **49**
**Meadway** MK41: Bed 1G **15**
**Mecca Bingo**
**Bedford** **5C 14**
**Medbury La.** MK42: Els 3C **26**
**Medmenham Av.** SG17: Chic 6D **36**
**Medusa Way** SG19: San 2B **20**
**Medway Cl.** MK45: Flit 2B **50**
**Meeting La.** SG19: Pot 4E **23**
**Megabowl**
**Bedford** **4E 15**
**Melbourne Cl.** SG5: Stot 4F **49**
**Melbourne St.**
MK42: Bed 6B **52** (4B **14**)
**Melrose Dr.** MK42: Els 2C **26**
**Mendham Way** MK45: Clop 2E **43**
**Mendip Cl.** MK45: Flit 2A **50**
**Mendip Cres.** MK41: Bed 1E **15**
**Mentmore Cl.** MK40: Bid 5D **12**
**Mepham Rd.** MK43: Woo 5B **24**
**MEPPERSHALL** **4F 45**
**Meppershall Rd.** SG16: U Sto 6H **45**
SG17: Mep 6E **45**
**Merchant La.** MK43: Cran 3A **32**
MK43: W End 2A **32**
**Merchants Ct.** MK42: Bed 5C **52**
**Mercury Pl.** SG17: Chic 5B **36**
**Merlin Dr.** SG19: San 1B **20**
**Merlin Gdns.** MK41: Bed 5C **6**
**Mersey Cl.** MK45: Flit 2B **50**
**Mersey Way** *MK41: Bed 4C 6*
*(off Wansbeck Rd.)*
**Merton Ho.**
MK40: Bed 1B **52** (2B **14**)
**Merton Rd.** MK40: Bed 1D **14**
**Mews, The**
MK40: Bed 2D **52** (2C **14**)
**Middlefield Ind. Est.**
SG19: San 2C **20**
**Middlefield La.** SG16: Hen 3E **47**
**Middleham Cl.** SG19: San 3C **20**
**Midland Cl.** SG17: Shef 6G **37**
**Midland Gdns.** SG17: Shef 6G **37**
**Midland Rd.**
MK40: Bed 4A **52** (3A **14**)
SG19: San 3B **20**
**Midland Structures Ind. Est.**
MK42: Bed 6A **14**
**Milburn Rd.** MK41: Bed 5H **7**
**Mile Rd.** MK42: Bed 1C **26**
(not continuous)
**Miles Dr.** SG17: Clif 6D **38**
**Millards Cl.** MK43: Cran 2C **32**
MK45: Flit 1B **50**
**Millards Pl.** MK43: Cran 2C **32**
**Millbrook Rd.** MK42: Bed 5B **14**
**Millbrook Station (Rail)** **6D 34**
**Mill Cl.** SG5: Stot 4G **49**
SG16: Hen 5F **39**
SG18: Big 4E **31**
**Miller Cl.** MK41: Clap 3E **5**
**Miller Ct.** MK42: Bed 1B **26**
**Miller Rd.** MK42: Bed 6B **14**
**Millers Ct.** SG18: Big 3E **31**
**Millfield** MK43: Brom 1B **12**
**Millfield Cl.** MK43: Cran 2B **32**
MK45: Flit 2E **51**
**Mill La.** MK42: Kem 1E **25**
MK45: Clop 1E **43**
MK45: Gre 2G **51**
MK45: H Con 5D **28**
SG5: Ast 1F **49**
SG5: Stot 4G **49**
SG15: Arl 6H **47**
SG17: Cam 2E **45**
SG18: Big 4E **31**
SG18: Lan 1G **39**
SG19: Eve, Pot 3B **22**
SG19: San 4B **20**
**Mill Mdw.** SG18: Lan 1G **39**
**Mill Rd.** MK43: Cran 2B **32**
SG18: Stan 2C **38**
**Millstream Ct.** SG17: Shef 5H **37**
**Mill St.** MK40: Bed 3C **52** (3C **14**)
**Mills Wlk.** SG19: San 3C **20**
**Millwood Ct.** SG5: Stot 4F **49**
**Millwright Way** MK45: Flit 6B **40**
**Mill Yd.** MK40: Bed 3C **52**
**Milne Row** MK40: Bed 2H **13**
**Milton Rd.** MK40: Bed 2H **13**
MK41: Clap 1E **5**
MK45: Flit 1A **50**
**Minden Cl.** MK45: Flit 6C **40**
**Mitford Cl.** MK41: Bed 5G **7**
**Mitre Cl.** MK41: Bed 2H **15**
**Mixies, The** SG5: Stot 4E **49**
**Moat Farm Barns**
MK43: M Mor 5A **34**
**Moat Farm Cl.** MK43: M Mor 5A **34**
MK45: Gre 2G **51**
**Mobbs Cl.** MK42: Kem 6F **13**
**MOGGERHANGER** **4E 19**
**Moggerhanger Pk.** **5D 18**
**Molivers La.** MK43: Brom 5A **4**
**Molly Moore Av.** MK42: Kem 2F **25**
**Monkshill** MK41: Bed 6G **7**
**Monmouth Cl.** MK42: Bed 6D **14**
**Monoux Pl.** SG19: San 4C **20**
**Monoux Rd.** MK43: Woo 6C **24**
**Montgomery Av.** SG17: Shef 1G **45**
**Montgomery Cl.** MK43: Stew 3G **35**
**Montgomery Ct.** MK42: Kem 6A **14**
**Moores Cl.** MK45: Mau 2E **43**
**Moorland Cl.** MK45: F'ton 1H **51**
**Moor La.** MK42: Bed 1D **26**
MK45: Flit 2E **51**
MK45: Mau 2G **41**
**Moor Pond Piece**
MK45: Amp 1B **40**
**Moors Vw. Cl.** MK45: Gre 2F **51**
**Moreteyne Rd.** MK43: M Mor 4A **34**
**Morgans Cl.** MK45: Wils 4F **29**
**Moriston Rd.** MK41: Bed 3C **6**
**Morland Way** MK41: Bed 6B **6**
**Morris Cl.** SG16: Hen 5E **47**
**Morris Gdns.** MK45: Amp 3B **40**
**Mortimer Rd.** MK42: Kem 5F **13**
**Moss La.** MK42: Els 4C **26**
**Moulton Av.** MK42: Bed 5E **15**
**Mountbatten Dr.** SG18: Big 2G **31**
**Mountbatten Pl.** MK41: Bed 2H **15**
**Mountbatten Way** SG17: Chic 4C **36**
**Mount Dr.** MK41: Bed 6G **7**
**Mt. Pleasant Rd.** MK41: Clap 3F **5**
**Mowbray Cl.** MK43: Brom 6A **4**
**Mowbray Cres.** SG5: Stot 3F **49**
**Mowbray Pl.** MK44: Will 2G **17**
**Mowbray Rd.** MK42: Bed 1C **26**
**Mowbrays, The** SG5: Stot 3F **49**
**Mowsbury Pk.** **3E 7**
**Mowsbury Wlk.** MK41: Bed 3D **6**
**Muirfield** MK40: Bid 5D **12**
**Mulberry Cl.** SG5: Stot 5F **49**
SG18: Big 1E **31**
**Mulberry Wlk.** MK42: Kem 2H **25**
**Murdock Rd.** MK41: Bed 5A **6**
**Murrell La.** SG5: Stot 5G **49**
**Muswell Rd.** MK42: Bed 6B **14**
**Myers Rd.** SG19: Pot 3D **22**
**Myrtle Rd.** MK42: Bed 6D **14**

## N

**Napier Rd.** MK41: Bed 6B **8**
**Naseby Pl.** MK45: Flit 5C **40**
**Nash Rd.** MK42: Bed 5E **15**
**Naylor Av.** MK42: Kem 3G **25**
**Neale Rd.** MK43: Woo 5B **24**
**Neale Way** MK43: Woo 5B **24**
**Neath Abbey** MK41: Bed 3H **15**
**Needwood Rd.** MK41: Bed 5H **7**
**Nelson Rd.** SG17: Chic 4C **36**
**Nelson St.** MK40: Bed 4H **13**
**Nene Rd.** MK45: Flit 2B **50**
SG16: Hen 6D **46**
**Neotsbury Ct.** *MK45: Amp 2D 40*
*(off Neotsbury Rd.)*
**Neotsbury Rd.** MK45: Amp 3D **40**
**Netherstones** SG5: Stot 3F **49**
**Nevern Gdns.** MK40: Bid 2F **13**
**Neville Cl.** MK43: Brom 1A **12**
**Neville Cres.** MK43: Brom 1A **12**
**Newark Av.** MK41: Bed 4G **7**
**Newbury Cl.** MK42: Kem 1F **25**
MK45: Sil 5D **42**
**Newbury Ct.** MK45: Sil 5D **42**
**Newbury Ho.** MK40: Bed 1D **14**
**Newbury La.** MK45: Sil 5D **42**
**Newis Cres.** SG17: Clif 6D **38**
**Newlands Rd.** MK45: Wes 6C **50**
**Newnham Av.** MK41: Bed 3E **15**
**Newnham Rd.**
MK40: Bed 3D **52** (3C **14**)
**Newnham St.**
MK40: Bed 3D **52** (3C **14**)
**New Rd.** MK43: Brom 2A **12**
MK44: G Bar 5C **10**
MK45: Mau 4F **41**
SG17: Clif 2C **46**
SG19: Bee, San 6C **20**
**Newstead Way** MK41: Bed 4F **7**
**New St.** SG17: Shef 6G **37**
**Newton Rd.** MK42: Bed 6C **14**
**Newton Way** SG19: San 3C **20**
**Newtown** SG16: Hen 5E **39**
SG19: Pot 4D **22**
**Newtown Ct.** SG18: Big 2G **31**
**Nicholls Cl.** *MK43: M Mor 4A 34*
*(off Beancroft Rd.)*
**Nicholls Rd.** MK42: Bed 5D **14**
**Nightingale Av.** MK41: Bed 4C **6**
**Nightingale M.** SG17: Shef 6G **37**
**Nimrod Dr.** SG17: Chic 4B **36**
**Nith Wlk.** *MK41: Bed 2C 6*
*(off Hodder Rd.)*
**Nodders Way** MK40: Bid 2E **13**
**Norfolk Cl.** MK41: Bed 3D **6**
**Norman Cl.** MK44: G Bar 4B **10**
**Normandy Cl.** MK42: Kem 6H **13**
**Normandy La.** SG18: Big 6H **31**
**Norse Rd.** MK41: Bed 5H **7**
**Northampton Rd.** MK43: Brom 6A **4**
**North Bri. St.** SG17: Shef 5G **37**
**Northcote** MK41: Bed 6G **7**
**Northcroft** SG19: San 4C **20**
**Northdale Cl.** MK42: Kem 1A **26**
**North Dr.** MK42: Sho 2G **27**
**North End** MK42: Sho 2G **27**
**Northfield Cl.** SG16: Hen 6F **39**
**Northfields** SG18: Big 2F **31**
**Northill Rd.** MK44: Cop 6E **17**
**North Pde.** MK40: Bed 2A **52**
**Northview** MK43: Brom 1A **12**
**Northwood End Rd.**
MK45: Hay 1A **36**
**Northwood La.** MK45: Wils 3G **29**
**Norton Rd.** SG5: Nor 6G **49**
SG5: Nor, Stot 6G **49**
**Nursery Cl.** MK45: Mau 2D **42**
SG18: Big 1G **31**
SG19: Pot 4C **22**
**Nursery Dr.** SG19: San 3A **20**
**Nursery Gdns.** MK41: Bed 5D **6**
**Nutwood Cl.** MK41: Bed 6A **8**

## O

**Oak Av.** MK45: Wils 5F **29**
**Oak Barn Cl.** MK43: Cran 3A **32**
**Oak Cl.** MK43: Woo 5C **24**
MK45: Wes 6C **50**
SG19: San 3B **20**
**Oak Cres.** SG18: Big 5G **31**
SG18: U Cal 1A **30**
SG19: Pot 4D **22**
**Oak Dr.** MK45: Pul 2H **51**
SG16: Hen 1F **47**
**Oak End** SG17: Shef 6A **38**
**Oaklands Rd.** MK40: Bed 1D **14**
**OAKLEY** **1B 4**
**Oakley Ri.** MK45: Wils 4E **29**
**Oakley Rd.** MK41: Clap 3D **4**
(not continuous)
MK43: Brom 4B **4**
**Oak Rd.** MK42: Bed 6D **14**
MK45: Flit 2D **50**
**Oaks, The** MK45: Sil 6E **43**
**Oaktree Rd.** MK45: Amp 3D **40**
**Oakwood Rd.** SG17: Shef 6H **37**
**Oasis Beach Pool** **4E 15**
**Oat Piece** MK43: M Mor 4B **34**
**Oberon Ct.** MK40: Bed 2A **14**
**Observer Cl.** MK40: Bid 2F **13**
**Oddie Coopers La.** SG19: San 1A **20**
**Odell Cl.** MK42: Kem 5F **13**
**Odin Cl.** MK41: Bed 5B **8**
**Offa Rd.** MK42: Bed 6B **14**
**Old Barn Cl.** SG16: Hen 6F **39**
**Old Barns, The** MK40: Bid 3D **12**
**Old Bedford Rd.** SG19: Pot 4D **22**
**Old Brewery Cl.** SG5: Stot 3F **49**
**Old Bri. Ct.** *SG17: Shef 6G 37*
*(off Old Bridge Way)*
**Old Bri. Way** SG17: Shef 6G **37**
**Old Church Path** MK45: Clop 1G **43**
**Oldfield Farm Rd.** SG16: Hen 6D **46**
(not continuous)
**Oldfield Rd.** MK40: Bed 4G **13**
**Old Ford End Rd.** MK40: Bed 4F **13**
**Old Harrowden Rd.**
MK42: Har 2F **27**
**Old Kiln La.** MK45: Clop 1E **43**
**Old M.** MK41: Bed 1A **52**
**Old Mill Cl.** SG18: Lan 1G **39**
**Old Mill La.** SG5: Shil 6B **44**
**Old Oak Cl.** SG15: Arl 2A **48**
**Old Oak Ind. Est.** SG15: Arl 2H **47**
**Old Oaks Dr.** MK40: Bid 3F **13**
**Old School Ct.** SG17: Clif 6D **38**
**Old School Gdns.** MK43: Woo 6B **24**
**Old School La.** SG18: Stan 1C **38**
**Old School Wlk.** SG15: Arl 6A **48**
**Old Silsoe Rd.** MK45: Clop 2E **43**
**Old Station Ct.** MK44: Blun 1F **19**
**Old Station Way** SG17: Shef 5G **37**
**Old Vicarage Gdns.**
SG16: Hen 6F **39**

*60 A-Z Bedford*

Oldways Rd.—Restormel Cl.


**Oldways Rd.** MK44: Rav 1F **7**
**Oliver's La.** SG5: Stot 3F **49**
**Oliver St.** MK45: Amp 2C **40**
**Olivier Ct.** MK40: Bed 2A **52**
**Olivier Way** SG17: Clif 6D **38**
**Olympus Rd.** SG16: Hen 6D **46**
**Ombersley Rd.** MK42: Bed 5B **14**
**Ongley Ct.** SG19: San 5D **20**
**Orchard Cl.** MK41: Bed 6E **7**
MK43: Brom 5B **4**
MK43: Cran 3A **32**
MK45: Grav 6A **44**
MK45: Wils 4E **29**
SG17: Mep 4G **45**
SG18: Big 3G **31**
SG19: Pot 4E **23**
**Orchard Dr.** SG17: Chic 6D **36**
**Orchard Rd.** SG19: Bee 6C **20**
**Orchards, The** MK45: Sil 6E **43**
**Orchard St.** MK42: Kem 2G **25**
**Orchard Way** MK43: Brom 2A **12**
MK43: Cran 3A **32**
MK44: G Bar 5C **10**
MK45: Flit 2D **50**
**Ormesby Way** MK40: Bed 4G **13**
**Orwell Cl.** MK41: Bed 4C **6**
**Osborn Cres.** SG17: Shef 6G **37**
**Osborne Av.** SG17: Chic 6C **36**
**Osborne Ct.** MK42: Bed 5B **14**
**Osier Link** MK45: Amp 3D **40**
**Osprey Cl.** MK42: Kem 3G **25**
SG19: San 1B **20**
**Osprey Rd.** MK45: Flit 2B **50**
**Ossory Pl.** MK45: Amp 2C **40**
**Ossory Way** MK42: Bed 5B **14**
**Othello Ct.** *MK40: Bed 1H **13***
*(off Shakespeare Rd.)*
**Otter Wlk.** MK41: Bed 4C **6**
**Ouseland Rd.** MK40: Bed 4G **13**
**Ouse Rd.** MK41: Bed 1G **15**
**Overdale** MK41: Bed 6G **7**
**Overlord Cl.** SG17: Shef 1G **45**
**Owen Cl.** MK42: Kem 2F **25**
*MK43: M Mor 4A **34***
*(off Arundel Rd.)*
**Owen Jones Cl.** SG16: Hen 5E **47**
**Owlswood** SG19: San 1B **20**
**Oxlip, The** MK45: Amp 1D **40**

## P

**Padbury Ho.** MK40: Bed 2A **14**
**Paddlers Ct.** MK40: Bed 4G **13**
**Paddock, The** MK40: Bid 3F **13**
**Paddock Cl.** MK41: Clap 2E **5**
**Paddocks, The** MK43: Brom 2B **12**
MK45: Flit 5B **40**
SG19: Pot 4D **22**
**Paddocks Chase** SG19: Pot 4D **22**
**Palace St.** SG18: Big 4F **31**
**Palgrave Rd.**
MK42: Bed 6A **52** (5A **14**)
**Palmer Cl.** SG17: Shef 5G **37**
**Palmerston St.**
MK41: Bed 1A **52** (1B **14**)
**Paradine Ct.**
MK40: Bed 3B **52** (3B **14**)
**Paradine Rd.** MK42: Bed 5D **14**
**Park & Ride**
**Dart** 4F **15**
**Elstow** 3A **26**
**Park Av.** MK40: Bed 1B **14**
**Park Cl.** MK44: Mog 5D **18**
**Park Ct.** SG19: San 5C **20**
**Park Cres.** MK43: Stew 2G **35**
**Park Farm Cl.** SG16: Hen 2F **47**
**Park Farm Ct.** MK41: Clap 3H **5**
**Park Hill** MK45: Amp 1C **40**
**Parklands** MK41: Bed 1F **15**
**Park La.** MK44: Blun 6G **11**
SG16: Hen 6F **39**
**Park La. Cres.** SG16: Hen 6F **39**
**Park Rd.** MK42: Kem 6H **13**
MK43: Stev 3A **4**
MK44: Mog 5D **18**
MK44: Rox 1G **11**
MK45: Wes 6C **50**
MK45: Wils 5E **29**
SG19: San 4C **20**
**Park Rd. Nth.** MK41: Bed 1B **14**
**Park Rd. W.**
MK41: Bed 1A **52** (1B **14**)
**Parkside** MK45: Grav 6A **44**
**Parkstone Cl.** MK41: Bed 3E **7**
**Park St.** MK45: Amp 1C **40**
**Park Vw.** MK44: Blun 6F **11**
**Parmiter Way** MK45: Amp 3B **40**
**Parrish Cl.** MK43: M Mor 4B **34**
**Parsonage Cl.** MK43: Oak 2C **4**
**Partridge La.** MK43: Brom 2A **12**
**Partridge Piece**
MK43: Cran 1C **32**
SG19: San 1B **20**
**Pastures, The** MK43: Stew 3G **35**
SG18: U Cal 1B **30**
**Pathway, The** MK45: Mau 1F **41**
**Patteshull Ct.** MK40: Bed 3A **52**
**Paula Radcliffe Way**
MK41: Bed 3E **5**
MK41: Clap 3E **5**
MK43: Brom 3E **5**
MK43: Oak 1D **4**
**Paul Waller Av.** MK44: Car 2H **27**
**Pavenham Rd.** MK43: Oak 1C **4**
**Pax Hill** MK41: Bed 5E **7**
**Payne Rd.** MK43: Woo 6B **24**
**Peacock Rd.** MK43: Brom 1A **12**
**Pearcey Rd.** MK42: Bed 6C **14**
**Pearmain Cl.** MK41: Bed 2F **15**
**Peartree Cl.** SG17: Shef 6A **38**
**Pear Tree Vw.** MK42: Els 3C **26**
**Peashill La.** MK44: G Bar 3B **10**
**Peckworth Ind. Est.**
SG16: L Sto 6C **46**
**Pedley La.** SG17: Clif 5B **38**
**Peel's Pl.** SG19: San 4D **20**
**Peel St.** MK40: Bed 2B **52** (2B **14**)
**Pegasus Ct.** SG18: Big 2E **31**
**Pegasus Dr.** SG18: Big 6H **31**
**Pemberley Av.** MK40: Bed 1C **14**
**Pemberley La.**
MK40: Bed 1D **52** (2C **14**)
**Pembroke Cl.** MK43: M Mor 4B **34**
**Pembroke Rd.** MK45: H Con 6D **28**
**Pembroke St.** MK40: Bed 3D **14**
**Pendennis Rd.** MK41: Bed 5G **7**
**Penfold Cl.** SG17: Shef 6E **37**
**Penlee Cl.** MK41: Bed 2F **15**
**Pennine Ri.** MK45: Flit 2B **50**
**Pennine Rd.** MK41: Bed 6E **7**
**Pennyfarthers Cl.** MK45: Mau 2D **42**
**Pentland Cl.** SG19: San 3B **20**
**Pentland Ri.** MK41: Bed 6E **7**
**Penwright Cl.** MK42: Kem 6F **13**
**Penwrights La.** MK44: G Bar 3B **10**
**Peppercorn Pk.** MK41: Clap 2H **5**
**Perkins Rd.** MK41: Bed 1A **16**
**Pershore Cl.** MK41: Bed 4E **7**
**Petley Cl.** MK45: Flit 3C **50**
**Petteril Wlk.** *MK41: Bed 2C **6***
*(off Carron Rd.)*
**Pevensey Gro.** MK45: Flit 3A **50**
**Pevensey Rd.** MK41: Bed 6G **7**
**Pheasant Wlk.** MK45: Flit 2B **50**
**Philip Larkin Ho.** *MK40: Bed 3A **14***
*(off The Avenue)*
**Phillpotts Av.** MK40: Bed 2E **15**
**Phipps Cl.** MK45: Wils 4F **29**
**Pickering Cl.** SG19: San 3C **20**
**Pilcroft St.**
MK42: Bed 6C **52** (4C **14**)
**Pilgrim Cen.** MK41: Bed 6D **6**
**Pilgrims Cl.** MK42: Bed 1C **26**
MK45: Flit 1C **50**
**Pilgrims Way** MK42: Bed 1C **26**
**Pillinge Rd.** MK43: Stew 3G **35**
**Pine Cl.** SG18: Big 2F **31**
**Pinemead** SG17: Shef 6A **38**
**Pines, The** MK42: Kem 2H **25**
MK45: Amp 2C **40**
**Pine Vw. Pk.** MK45: Mau 3D **42**
**Pinsent Av.** MK43: Brom 2A **12**
**Pioneer Pk.** MK42: Bed 6B **14**
**Pipit Cl.** MK45: Flit 2C **50**
**Pipit Gro.** SG19: San 1B **20**
**Pipit Ri.** MK41: Bed 5C **6**
**Pix Ct.** SG15: Arl 2A **48**
**Pix Rd.** SG5: Stot 5E **49**
**Place, The** 2D **14**
**Planes, The** MK42: Kem 2G **25**
**Playfield Cl.** SG18: Big 4G **31**
**Pleasant Pl.** SG19: San 4C **20**
**Plough Cl.** MK43: Cran 4A **32**
**Plovers Fld.** SG19: San 1B **20**
**Plover Way** MK41: Bed 5B **6**
**Polhill Av.** MK41: Bed 1D **14**
**Pollards Cl.** MK45: Wils 4E **29**
**Polo Fld. Way** MK42: Kem 3H **25**
**Pope Cl.** *MK45: Flit 3C **50***
*(off Vicarage Hill)*
**Popes Way** MK43: Woo 6A **24**
**Poplar Av.** MK41: Bed 4E **7**
MK45: Wils 5F **29**
**Poplar Cl.** MK44: Rox 2G **11**
MK45: Sil 6E **43**
SG18: Big 1F **31**
SG19: San 4A **20**
**Poplar Dr.** SG5: Stot 2F **49**
**Poplars, The** MK45: Amp 2D **40**
SG15: Arl 2A **48**
**Poppy Fld.** SG18: Big 4H **31**
**Poppyfields** MK41: Bed 5A **8**
**Portia Ho.** MK40: Bed 2A **14**
**Portland Cl.** MK41: Bed 1G **15**
**Portnall Pl.** MK43: Cran 2C **32**
**Postley Rd.** MK42: Kem 3F **25**
**Potters Cross** MK43: Woo 6C **24**
**Potter Way** MK42: Bed 1C **26**
**POTTON** 4E **23**
**Potton Rd.** SG18: Big 2F **31**
SG19: Eve 1A **22**
SG19: Gam 2D **22**
SG19: San 5D **20**
**Poulter Cl.**
MK40: Bed 4A **52** (3B **14**)
**Pound, The** MK45: Wes 6C **50**
**Pound Cl.** MK43: Cran 3B **32**
MK44: Blun 5G **11**
SG18: Lan 1G **39**
SG18: U Cal 1A **30**
**Powells Rd.** SG17: Shef 5G **37**
**Powers Cl.** SG19: San 2B **20**
**Powis M.** *MK45: Flit 3B **50***
*(off Conway Dr.)*
**Powis Rd.** MK41: Bed 5H **7**
**Prebend St.**
MK40: Bed 4A **52** (3B **14**)
**Premier Health & Fitness Club** 1A **16**
**Prentice Gdns.** MK42: Kem 6G **13**
**Preservine Wlk.** MK41: Clap 4G **5**
**Preston Cl.** MK45: Amp 2C **40**
**Preston Rd.** MK40: Bed 3H **13**
**Prestwick Rd.** MK40: Bid 3D **12**
**Primary Way** SG15: Arl 6A **48**
**Primrose Cl.** MK43: M Mor 5A **34**
MK45: Flit 2B **50**
SG15: Arl 6H **47**
SG18: Big 5H **31**
**Primrose La.** SG15: Arl 6H **47**
**Princes Rd.** MK43: Brom 1A **12**
**Princess St.** MK40: Bed 1B **52**
MK41: Clap 3F **5**
**Princes St.**
MK40: Bed 1B **52** (2B **14**)
SG5: Stot 3F **49**
**Princeton Ct.** MK41: Bed 6C **6**
**Prinknash Rd.** MK41: Bed 4E **7**
**Printers Ct.** MK45: Amp 1D **40**
**Prior Cl.** MK41: Clap 2E **5**
**Priory Bus. Pk.** MK44: Bed 5A **16**
**Priory Country Pk.** 4G **15**
**Priory Country Pk. Vis. Cen.** 4G **15**
**Priory Ct.** MK40: Bed 2A **52**
**Priory Ga.** SG17: Shef 6E **37**
**Priory Rd.** SG17: Cam 6D **36**
**Priory Sailing Club** 4G **15**
**Priory St.**
MK40: Bed 3A **52** (3B **14**)
**Priory Ter.** MK40: Bed 2A **52**
**Proctor Cl.** MK42: Kem 6F **13**
**Progress Pk.** MK42: Els 3A **26**
**Progress Way** MK42: Els 1B **26**
**Prospect Pl.** SG18: Big 5E **31**
**Prospect Rd.** SG18: Lan 2H **39**
**Prudden Cl.** MK42: Els 1B **26**
**Pryor Gdns.** SG5: Stot 3F **49**
**PULLOXHILL** 4H **51**
**Pulloxhill Bus. Pk.** MK45: Pul 2H **51**
**Pullox Hill Rd.** MK45: Gre 2G **51**
**Purbeck Cl.** MK41: Bed 1G **15**
**Purcell Way** SG17: Shef 5A **38**
**PUTNOE** 5F **7**
**Putnoe Hgts.** MK41: Bed 5F **7**
**Putnoe La.** MK41: Bed 6E **7**
**Putnoe St.** MK41: Bed 5F **7**
**Pyghtle, The** MK45: Grav 6A **44**
MK45: Wes 6C **50**
**Pyms Cl.** MK44: G Bar 4B **10**
**Pym's Way** SG19: San 2B **20**

## Q

**Quantock Cl.** MK41: Bed 1E **15**
**Quantocks, The** MK45: Flit 2B **50**
**Quantrelle Ct.** *MK42: Sho 3G **27***
*(off South Dr.)*
**Queen Alexandra Rd.**
MK41: Bed 2G **15**
**Queen Anne's Cl.** SG5: Stot 5F **49**
**Queen Elizabeth Cl.**
SG17: Shef 6H **37**
**Queensbury Cl.** MK40: Bed 3H **13**
**Queens Cl.** MK40: Bid 2F **13**
MK43: Oak 1B **4**
MK45: Flit 2D **50**
**Queens Ct.**
MK40: Bed 1B **52** (2B **14**)
SG17: Shef 6H **37**
**Queens Cres.** MK41: Bed 6F **7**
MK41: Clap 2F **5**
**Queen's Dr.** MK41: Bed 5F **7**
**QUEEN'S PARK** 3H **13**
**Queens Rd.** MK45: Amp 2D **40**
SG19: San 4B **20**
**Queen St.** MK40: Bed 1A **52** (2B **14**)
SG5: Stot 5G **49**
**Quenby Way** MK43: Brom 1B **12**
**Quince Ct.** *SG19: San 2B **20***
*(off Engayne Av.)*

## R

**Race Mdws. Way** MK42: Kem 3H **25**
**Radnor Wlk.** MK41: Bed 6H **7**
**RADWELL** 6H **49**
**Radwell La.** SG7: Rad 6H **49**
**Raglan Ct.** *MK41: Bed 4G **7***
*(off Devizes Av.)*
**Raglan Grn.** MK41: Bed 5G **7**
**Railton Rd.** MK42: Kem 4F **25**
**Railway Cotts.** MK43: Oak 1C **4**
**Railway Vw.** SG18: Big 3F **31**
**Raleigh St.** MK40: Bed 4H **13**
**Rally, The** SG15: Arl 3A **48**
(not continuous)
**Ramillies Cl.** MK42: Kem 6H **13**
**Ramsay Cl.** MK41: Bed 6B **6**
**Ramsey Cl.** MK42: Kem 3F **25**
**Ram Yd.** MK40: Bed 3C **52** (3C **14**)
SG15: Arl 6A **48**
**Randalls Cl.** MK43: Brom 1B **12**
**Ranworth Wlk.** MK40: Bed 4F **13**
**Ravensden Rd.** MK41: Ren 1G **7**
**Raven Wlk.** MK45: Flit 2C **50**
**Rays Cl.** MK42: Bed 5D **52** (4C **14**)
**Readshill** MK45: Clop 2E **43**
**Recreation Ri.** MK45: Grav 6A **44**
**Rectory Cl.** SG17: Clif 5D **38**
**Rectory Ct.** SG19: San 4C **20**
**Rectory Farm Bus. Pk.**
SG16: U Sto 6H **45**
**Rectory La.** MK43: Cran 4B **32**
MK45: Amp 1D **40**
MK45: H Con 6C **28**
**Rectory Rd.** SG17: Cam 1D **44**
SG17: Mep 5F **45**
**Redborne Tennis Courts** 5C **40**
**Redborne Upper School & Community Sports Hall** 4C **40**
**Reddall Cl.** MK42: Bed 6F **15**
**Rede Cl.** MK41: Bed 3C **6**
**Redhills Cl.** MK45: Mau 2B **42**
**Red Lion Cl.** MK43: Cran 3B **32**
**Redman Gdns.** SG18: Big 2F **31**
**Redwald Cl.** MK42: Kem 1G **25**
**Redwood Gro.** MK42: Bed 5C **14**
**Regent Cl.** MK41: Bed 3C **6**
**Regent Ct.** *MK40: Bed 2H **13***
*(off Shakespeare Rd.)*
SG5: Stot 3F **49**
**Regents M.** MK40: Bid 3E **13**
**Regent St.** SG5: Stot 4E **49**
**Rendlesham Wlk.** MK41: Bed 6A **8**
**RENHOLD** 3C **8**
**Renhold Rd.** MK44: Wild 1C **8**
**Repton Cl.** MK41: Bed 5F **7**
**Repton Rd.** SG17: Chic 4C **36**
**Restormel Cl.** MK41: Bed 4F **7**

**Water End** MK41: Ren .........5E 9
  MK44: Cop .............6E 17
  MK45: Mau ............4A 42
**Water La.** MK41: Ren .........6F 9
  MK42: Kem ...........2E 25
  MK45: Flit .............2D 50
**Waterloo Cl.** MK45: Flit ......6C 40
**Waterloo Rd.**
  MK40: Bed ......4D 52 (3C 14)
**Waters End** SG5: Stot ........4E 49
**Watkin Wlk.** SG18: Big ........2E 31
**Watson Rd.** MK45: Wils ......1B 28
**Watson Way** MK43: M Mor ....4B 34
**Wavell Cl.** MK43: Stew .......4G 35
  (not continuous)
**Waveney Av.** MK41: Bed .......5C 6
**Waverley Av.** SG19: San ......2B 20
**Wear, The** MK41: Bed ........2C 6
**Weaver Cl.** MK41: Bed ........3D 6
**Weavers Grn.** SG19: San ......1C 20
**Weavers Orchard** SG15: Arl ...6A 48
**Webber Cl.** SG17: Shef ........5H 37
**Webbs Cl.** MK43: Brom .......1B 12
**Wedgwood Rd.** MK41: Bed .....6B 6
**Weedon Cl.** SG16: Hen .......5E 47
**Welbeck Gdns.** MK41: Bed ....4F 7
**Welbourne Gdns.** MK42: Bed ..6F 15
**Wellington Cl.** MK40: Bed ....1B 52
**Wellington Dr.** SG17: Chic ....5D 36
**Wellington Rd.** MK42: Sho ....3F 27
**Wellington St.**
  MK40: Bed ......1B 52 (2B 14)
**Wells Cl.** MK42: Kem .........5G 13
**Wellsfield** MK44: Blun ........6G 11
**Wendover Ct.** MK41: Bed .....2F 15
**Wendover Dr.** MK41: Bed .....2F 15
**Wenlock Rd.** MK42: Kem ......2E 25
**Wentworth Dr.** MK41: Bed .....4E 7
  (not continuous)
**Wesley Cl.** SG15: Arl .........6A 48
**Wesley Rd.** SG19: San .......2C 20
**Westbourne Rd.** MK40: Bed ...3H 13
**Westbury Ct.** *MK41: Bed* .......*4C 6*
  *(off Torridge Ri.)*
**West Ct.** MK41: Bed .........1G 15
**Westdale Wlk.** MK42: Kem ....1H 25
**West Dr.** SG15: Arl ..........6A 48
**WEST END** ...............4A 32
**West End** MK42: Els .........2A 26
**West End La.** SG19: Pot .......3E 23
**West End Rd.** MK43: Bed .....6A 12
  MK45: Sil ..............6D 42
**Western St.**
  MK40: Bed ......4A **52** (3B **14**)
**Western Way** SG19: San ......3B 20
**Westfield Gdns.** SG19: San ...3B 20
**Westfield Rd.** MK40: Bed .....3H 13
  MK43: Oak ...........1A 4
  SG16: Hen ............1E 47
**West Gro.** MK40: Bed ........3H 13

**Westminster Gdns.**
  MK42: Kem ...........6G 13
**WESTONING** ..............6C 50
**Westoning Rd.** MK45: Gre .....4E 51
**Westoria Ct.** *MK45: Wes* ......*6C 50*
  *(off Park Rd.)*
**West Rd.** SG19: San ..........4B 20
**Westrope Way** MK41: Bed .....2D 6
**West Vw.** SG18: Lan .........2H 39
  SG19: Bee .............6B 20
**Westview** MK43: Brom .......1A 12
**West Wlk.** SG18: Big .........2G 31
**West Way** MK44: Mog ........4E 19
**Westwood Cl.** MK42: Sho .....3G 27
**Wharf, The** MK41: Bed ........3C 6
**Wharfe, The** MK41: Bed ......3C 6
**Wharf M.** SG18: Big ..........3E 31
**Wheathouse Cl.** MK41: Bed ....5F 7
**Wheatlands Cl.** MK45: Mau ....2A 42
**Whinnett's Way** MK45: Pul ....3H 51
**Whiston Cres.** SG17: Clif ......5D 38
**Whitbeam Cl.** MK42: Kem .....3H 25
**Whitbread Av.** MK42: Bed .....5A 14
**Whitby Way** MK42: Els ........2C 26
**Whitecrofts** SG5: Stot .........3E 49
**White Lodge Cl.** MK42: Kem ...2E 25
**Whiteman Cl.** SG18: Lan ......3H 39
**Whitestones** SG19: Bee .......6C 20
**Whitings** MK40: Bid ...........5D 12
**Whitley Rd.** MK42: Sho .......2G 27
**Whittingstall Av.** MK42: Kem ..1H 25
**Whittle Cl.** SG16: Hen ........6D 46
**Whitworth Ct.** MK42: Kem ....1G 25
  *SG17: Shef* ............*5G 37*
  *(off High St.)*
**Whitworth Jones Av.**
  SG16: Hen ...........5E 47
**Whitworth Way** MK45: Wils ....3F 29
**Widecombe Cl.** MK40: Bed ....1E 15
**Wigram Cl.** MK42: Els ........1B 26
**Wilden Rd.** MK41: Ren .......3H 7
**Wildflower Way** MK42: Bed ....1F 27
**Williamson Cl.** MK42: Kem ....3E 25
**Williamson Rd.** MK42: Kem ....3E 25
**William Sutton Ct.**
  MK40: Bed ...........3A 52
**Williams Way** MK45: Flit .......5B 40
**WILLINGTON** .............3G 17
**Willington Rd.** MK44: Cop .....4E 17
**Willmers Cl.** MK42: Kem .......5E 7
**Willoughby Cl.** MK44: G Bar ...4B 10
**Willow Cl.** MK43: Brom .......6B 4
  MK45: Sil .............5D 42
**Willow Ri.** SG19: San .........5D 20
**Willow Rd.** MK42: Bed .......6D 14
  MK45: Wils ...........5E 29
  SG19: Pot .............4E 23
**Willows, The** MK43: Woo .....5C 24
  MK45: Flit .............1C 50
**Willow Springs** MK43: Cran ....4A 32

**Willow Trees Cvn. Site**
  SG16: L Sto .............6C 46
**Willow Way** MK45: Amp .......3D 40
  MK45: Flit .............3D 50
**Willsheres Rd.** SG18: Big ......2E 31
**Wilmon Ct.** SG18: Lan ........3G 39
**WILSTEAD** ................3F 29
**Wilstead Ind. Pk.** MK45: Wils ..1C 28
**Wilstead Rd.** MK42: Els .......2C 26
**Winchester Rd.** MK42: Bed ....1E 27
  SG19: San ............2C 20
**Windermere, The** MK42: Kem ..2F 25
**Windermere Cl.** MK45: Flit ....2C 50
**Windermere Dr.** SG18: Big .....5F 31
**Windmill Hill** MK40: Bid .......6H 7
**Windmill Rd.** MK45: Flit .......1B 50
**Windmill Vw.** SG18: Big .......5F 31
**Windmill Way** MK43: Cran .....1C 32
**Windrush Av.** MK41: Bed ......4C 6
**Windrush Cl.** MK45: Flit .......2B 50
**Windsor Cl.** MK45: Flit ........3B 50
**Windsor Ct.** MK42: Bed .......1D 26
**Windsor Gdns.** MK40: Bed .....1D 14
**Windsor Rd.** MK42: Bed .......6D 14
**Windsor Way** SG18: Lan .......2H 39
  SG19: San ............4C 20
**Wingate Dr.** MK45: Amp .......2D 40
**Wingfield Av.** MK45: Mau ......1F 41
**Wingfield Cl.** MK40: Bed ......4G 13
**Wingfield Ct.** MK45: Amp ......2D 40
**Wingfield Dr.** SG19: Pot .......3E 23
**Wingfield Rd.** MK43: Brom ....5B 4
**Winifred Rd.** MK40: Bed .......3H 13
**Winston Cres.** SG18: Big .......2F 31
**Wisdom Cl.** MK43: Brom ......1A 12
**Wisson Cl.** MK45: Wils ........3F 29
**Witham Cl.** MK41: Bed ........2D 6
**Withybrook** *MK45: Flit* ...........*1C 50*
  *(off Steppingley Rd.)*
**Woburn Cl.** MK45: Flit .........3A 50
**Woburn Cl.** *MK42: Kem* .........*2F 25*
  *(off St John's Av.)*
**Woburn Rd.** MK40: Bed .......3A 14
  MK42: Kem ...........4F 25
  MK43: Kem, Woo ......6D 24
  MK43: M Mor ..........5A 34
  MK45: Amp, Mil ........1A 40
**Woburn Rd. Ind. Est.**
  MK42: Kem ...........4G 25
  (Adams Cl.)
  MK42: Kem ...........4F 25
  (Wolseley Rd.)
**Woburn St.** MK45: Amp .......1C 40
**Wolseley Bus. Pk.**
  MK42: Kem ...........4G 25
**Wolseley Ct.** MK42: Kem ......4F 25
**Wolseley Rd.** MK42: Kem .....4F 25
**Woodall Cl.** SG18: Big ........3E 31

**Wood Cl.** MK40: Bid .........2E 13
**Woodcock Cl.** SG19: San .....1B 20
**Woodcock Wlk.** *MK45: Flit* ....*3B 50*
  *(off Larkway)*
**Woodcote** MK41: Bed .........6F 7
**WOOD END** ................5F 33
**Wood End La.** MK45: Wils .....3A 24
**Woodend La.** MK44: G Bar ....1E 11
**Wood End Rd.** MK43: Cran ....6B 32
  MK43: Kem ...........4A 24
**Woodfield La.** MK41: Ren .....4E 9
**Woodland Cl.** SG19: Pot .......3E 23
**Woodland Dr.** MK43: Brom ....5B 4
  MK45: Wils ...........5F 29
**Woodland Pk.** MK45: Wils .....5F 29
**Woodlands** MK41: Clap .......5B 8
**Woodlands, The** SG18: Bro ....6B 30
**Woodlands Cl.** MK44: Cop .....6E 17
**Wood La.** MK41: Ren .........2C 8
  MK44: Will ............3H 11
**Woodmere** MK41: Bed ........6F 7
**Woodpecker Way** SG19: San ...1B 20
**WOODSIDE** ................4G 7
**Woodstock Rd.** MK40: Bed ....5H 13
**Woodview** MK45: Wils .........5F 29
**Woodville Dr.** MK40: Bid ......5D 12
**Woolfield** SG19: San ..........5D 20
**WOOTTON** ................6B 24
**WOOTTON GREEN** .........1B 34
**Wootton Rd.** MK44: Kem ......4C 24
**Worcester Rd.** MK42: Bed .....1F 27
**Wordsworth Cl.** SG18: U Cal ...1B 30
**Wordsworth Ct.** MK40: Bed ....1H 13
**WORKHOUSE END** .........4E 9
**Wrayfields** SG5: Stot .........3H 49
**Wren Cl.** MK45: Flit ..........3B 50
  SG19: San ............2C 20
**Wrest House** ..............6G 43
**Wrestlingworth Rd.**
  SG19: Pot .............5G 23
**Wrest Pk.** MK45: Sil ..........6E 43
**Wroxham Way** MK40: Bed .....4F 13
**Wyatt Rd.** MK42: Kem .........2F 25
**Wychwood Rd.** MK41: Bed .....5H 7
**Wycklond Cl.** SG5: Stot .......4E 49
**Wye Cl.** MK41: Bed ...........4D 6
**Wynchwood La.** SG17: Shef ....6F 37
**Wynnefield Wlk.** SG19: San ....3C 20
**Wyton Ct.** SG17: Chic ........6D 36

# Y

**Yeomans Ga.** MK44: Car ......6B 16
**Yew Tree Wlk.** SG17: Clif .....6D 38
**Yew Wlk.** MK45: Amp .........3E 41
**York Cl.** SG18: Big ...........4G 31
**York St.** MK40: Bed ..........2E 15